# THE LIVING WORD

*An Introduction to Old Testament Theology*

# UNDERSTANDING THE BIBLE

Edited by EDGAR JONES, M.A., B.D., Ph.D.,
Principal of the Congregational College, Manchester

*A series of six volumes designed for the use of students in Colleges of Education, Universities and Theological Colleges. Also suitable for students in the senior forms of Secondary schools.*

## 1. THE TESTIMONY OF ISRAEL
Harry Mowvley, M.A.    Special Lecturer in Hebrew, University of Bristol; member of B.C.C. Theological Advisory Committee; Tutor, Bristol Baptist College.

## 2. THE FEAR OF THE LORD
Roger Tomes, M.A., B.D.    Member of the Society for Old Testament Studies; formerly Tutor at New College, London; Minister, Whitefield Memorial Church, London.

## 3. THE LIVING WORD
Edgar Jones, M.A., B.D., Ph.D.    Principal of Congregational College, Manchester; Hon. Lecturer in Biblical Studies in University of Manchester; Extra-Mural Lecturer for Universities of Manchester and Liverpool; Member of Society for Old Testament Studies.

## 4. THE WORLD OF THE NEW TESTAMENT
Derrick J. Bowden, B.A., B.D.    Senior Lecturer in Divinity, Padgate College of Education; formerly teacher in various Secondary schools.

## 5. THE LITERATURE OF THE NEW TESTAMENT
W. Gordon Robinson, M.A., B.D., Ph.D.    Formerly Principal of Northern Congregational College, Manchester; formerly Lecturer in New Testament, University of Manchester; Lecturer in Ecclesiastical History, University of Manchester.

## 6. THE MESSAGE OF THE NEW TESTAMENT
J. H. E. Hull, M.A., B.D.    Senior Lecturer, Congregational College, Manchester; Lecturer in New Testament Studies, University of Manchester.

# THE LIVING WORD

*An Introduction to Old Testament Theology*

BY

EDGAR JONES

THE RELIGIOUS EDUCATION PRESS, LTD.

*(A member of the Pergamon Group)*

HEADINGTON HILL HALL, OXFORD

Pergamon Press Ltd., Headington Hill Hall, Oxford

Pergamon Press Inc., Maxwell House, Fairview Park, Elmsford, New York 10523

Pergamon of Canada Ltd., 207 Queen's Quay West, Toronto 1

Pergamon Press (Aust.) Pty. Ltd., 19a Boundary Street,
Rushcutters Bay, N.S.W. 2011, Australia

Vieweg & Sohn GmbH, Burgplatz 1, Braunschweig

---

First edition 1970

Library of Congress Catalog Card No. 76–115401

*Printed in Great Britain by A. Wheaton & Co., Exeter*

08 016343 2 (flexicover)
08 015539 1 (hard cover)

# CONTENTS

# ABBREVIATIONS

*Abbreviations used in this series for the books of the Bible*

## OLD TESTAMENT

| | | | |
|---|---|---|---|
| Gen | Genesis | Eccles | Ecclesiastes |
| Ex | Exodus | Song | Song of Solomon |
| Lev | Leviticus | Is | Isaiah |
| Num | Numbers | Jer | Jeremiah |
| Deut | Deuteronomy | Lam | Lamentations |
| Josh | Joshua | Ezek | Ezekiel |
| Judg | Judges | Dan | Daniel |
| Ruth | Ruth | Hos | Hosea |
| 1 Sam | 1 Samuel | Joel | Joel |
| 2 Sam | 2 Samuel | Amos | Amos |
| 1 Kings | 1 Kings | Obad | Obadiah |
| 2 Kings | 2 Kings | Jon | Jonah |
| 1 Chron | 1 Chronicles | Mic | Micah |
| 2 Chron | 2 Chronicles | Nahum | Nahum |
| Ezra | Ezra | Hab | Habakkuk |
| Neh | Nehemiah | Zeph | Zephaniah |
| Esther | Esther | Hag | Haggai |
| Job | Job | Zech | Zechariah |
| Ps | Psalms | Mal | Malachi |
| Prov | Proverbs | | |

## NEW TESTAMENT

| | | | |
|---|---|---|---|
| Mt | Matthew | 1 Tim | 1 Timothy |
| Mk | Mark | 2 Tim | 2 Timothy |
| Lk | Luke | Tit | Titus |
| Jn | John | Philem | Philemon |
| Acts | Acts of the Apostles | Heb | Hebrews |
| Rom | Romans | Jas | James |
| 1 Cor | 1 Corinthians | 1 Pet | 1 Peter |
| 2 Cor | 2 Corinthians | 2 Pet | 2 Peter |
| Gal | Galatians | 1 Jn | 1 John |
| Eph | Ephesians | 2 Jn | 2 John |
| Phil | Philippians | 3 Jn | 3 John |
| Col | Colossians | Jude | Jude |
| 1 Thess | 1 Thessalonians | Rev | Revelation |
| 2 Thess | 2 Thessalonians | | |

## ACKNOWLEDGEMENT

THE scripture quotations in this publication are from the Revised Standard Version of the Bible copyrighted 1946 and 1952 by the Division of Christian Education, National Council of Churches and used by permission.

# PREFACE

ONE of the marked features of Bible study in recent years, has been the revival of interest in Old Testament Theology. The question is asked again and again, What does the Old Testament say? This is distinct from a study of isolated verses or a study of separate religious ideas. It is possible, we believe, to offer an account of the theology of the Old Testament as a whole, as it emerges through a study of the persons and events that form its history.

Underlying this approach is the principle of the unity of the Bible. Old and New Testaments are integrally connected. The Old Testament is concerned with the same saving purpose, whose fulfilment is the subject of the New Testament.

The frequent quotation of the actual words of the text is based on the conviction that the reader will gain from hearing the words speak for themselves. I have been greatly helped in the preparation of this volume by the co-operation of the Rev. Roger Tomes and the Rev. Harry Mowvley who read it in typescript and made valuable comments and suggestions. It is my pleasure to express my appreciation of the continued stimulus and encouragement of the Rev. Gordon K. Hawes, Chief Editor of the Religious Education Press.

EDGAR JONES

xi

# PART ONE

# INTRODUCTION

# 1

# THE BIBLE AND THEOLOGY

## THE NATURE OF BIBLICAL THEOLOGY

The words 'Bible' and 'Theology' are certainly loaded terms. What do we mean by 'Biblical Theology'? A working definition is—the study of the religious ideas of the Bible within their historical context. This will do as our starting point, but we must hasten to add three further characteristics of our quest.

*We are more concerned with living relationships than the dry descriptions of a museum catalogue*

The function of the discipline that we call Biblical Theology is to describe the ways in which the Bible thinks of God, of man and of their relationship together. This will include views of the world, physical and social, of the individual and society, of life and death. Yet we are not listing items that can be tabulated and dissected as some butterfly specimen, under a glass case. The ideas we shall examine are the direct outcome of the experience of living men and women who belong to a community and only from within such a community and fellowship can the ideas be themselves discovered and then assessed. The aim of the Bible theologian is to communicate life not catalogue antiquities.

3

### We are approaching the Bible as a Unity

This means that we cannot deal with the Old Testament as if
the New Testament never existed. It is from within the continuing
New Testament community, that is, the Church, that we
approach the Old Testament with the presupposition that the
Old Testament is nothing less than Christian Scripture. What
we are really going to study is the biblical theology of the Old
Testament, the beginnings of the record of the experience that is
continued in the New Testament and through our present-day
witness is an unfinished story.

### We see Old Testament Theology as both Crown and Bridge

By these two metaphors we mean just this. There are many
fields of Old Testament study such as the study of the history of
the Hebrews, of their religious ideas and institutions, of the impact
of the Ancient Near Eastern culture upon their life, the stimulus
afforded by all the recent archaeological research, and the
examination of the language characteristics of the Hebrews now
enriched by our increasing knowledge of the documents of the
Ancient world. All these disciplines or fields of study are indis-
pensable for the student of the Old Testament and make a real
contribution to our understanding of it.

The relevance of Old Testament theology is that all the results
of such monumental labours are used to answer the ultimate
question that every generation must ask—what was the purpose of
God in bringing into being his Covenant People? This is the
crowning question and quest. To ask in effect, what is it all
about? This is an issue that we might not want to raise but we
cannot here retire to the sidelines because through the very

affirmations, we shall later discover, we are already involved. The word of the Bible theologian is eventually 'Choose!' Not 'Consider at your leisure, if you are so minded!'

Old Testament theology is the bridge along which those who have laboured to discover the historical truth, the cultural background and the linguistic treasures must travel to use their riches in the fuller understanding of what it means to share in the life of the One who became the Living Word.

## THE TRUTH AND AUTHORITY OF THE BIBLE

Because we have no right as Bible students to look at our material in a cultural vacuum or rarefied ecclesiastical atmosphere, we are bound to give answers to two further questions: Is the Bible true? and What is its Authority?

A valid comment on the question of the Bible's truth has been made: 'One cannot close one's eyes to the fact that the Old Testament contains many statements of historical, geographical, chronological, and biological nature, and so on, that simply cannot be harmonised with the present stage of our knowledge, statements which, therefore, to that extent are *erroneous*' (Sigmund Mowinckel, *The Old Testament as Word of God*, p. 13). The straight issue is—can there be mistakes in that which we have called the 'Word of God'? We must note immediately that this must not be equated with saying or even suggesting that God made all these mistakes and doesn't know his job! The more we examine the Bible and the way in which it came into being, the way that records were made and then transmitted, the extension of human knowledge and the fallibility of language to convey fully the deepest experiences, the only conclusion we come to is this—that instead of reluctantly admitting with something of shame that there are errors and inconsistencies, we thank God that it is such a human book and see that mistakes are inevitable and part of the way in which God chose to make his will and purpose known.

We can yet affirm that the Bible is both human, and so at points containing error, and still an inspired instrument of God. Clearly we must give up any idea of inspiration that is mechanical in its operation—as if God, for example, ever spoke to the prophets as if they were glorified stenographers required to produce copies of his message to them in triplicate by the next morning! Instead of this view of inspiration that reduces the urgency of prophecy to something akin to magic we would welcome the comment that 'The authority of their words does not rest upon the specific wording, nor upon the "infallibility" of the form or of any detail, but upon the fact that the ideas are given them by God for just *that* moment and just *that* situation in which they find themselves' (S. Mowinckel, *The Old Testament as Word of God*, p. 26).

They had the authority of their own experience that derived from a relationship with the Living God, who spoke to real men in real situations and so they could do no other! To the truth of this belief let one of their number himself bear witness:

> 'If I say, "I will not mention him, or speak any more in his name,"
>     there is in my heart as it were a burning fire
> shut up in my bones,
>     and I am weary with holding it in, and I cannot' (Jer. 20.9).

## THE OLD TESTAMENT AS WORD OF GOD

The Old Testament is to be seen not as a mere collection of the religious ideas of the Israelites, but as the source to which we must ever return for our knowledge of the coming into existence of the covenant community which is continued in the church of

New Testament times which is rightly called the New Israel (Gal. 6.*16*).

This is not to dismiss the Old Testament as just a 'pre-view' of the real revelation of God in Jesus Christ but a realisation that although it is never to be relegated to an unreal, shadowy status as if God was making just a trial run, the revelation of God, to which the Old Testament bears its witness, is partial and incomplete.

'Speaking figuratively, we may say that the events of the Old Testament are like the first two acts of a play, incomplete in themselves without the final act. We should also say that though the events of the New Testament contain the crisis and dénouement of the final act, they cannot be fully understood without the first two acts. The Early Church understood the Old Testament in this light. We should never forget that the Old Testament was the Holy Scripture of the Early Church—the only Scripture it had at first. It was the Bible of Jesus and Paul' (Dwight E. Stevenson, *Preaching on the Books of the Old Testament*, p. 6).

The essential relationship between the Old and New Testaments may be summarised in three basic principles we can briefly illustrate:

### The Old Testament was the Heritage of Jesus and His Disciples

When Jesus wanted to find words to express what he believed his life role to be he turned to the Servant Songs of Second Isaiah (Is. 53.*12*) and spoke of giving his life as a ransom for many (Mk. 10.*45*). The challenge of his Temptation struggle is met by his reliance upon the spiritual sustenance afforded by the words of Deuteronomy:

> You shall fear the Lord your God; you shall serve him, and swear by his name. . . . You shall not put the Lord your God to the test, as you tested him at Massah (Deut. 6.*13,16*).

Similarly, the term that is used by Jesus to describe himself comes from the Old Testament:

> I saw in the night visions, and behold, with the clouds of heaven
> there came one like a son of man,
> and he came to the Ancient of Days
> and was presented before him (Dan. 7.*13*).

Again and again in the New Testament we find this self-description used by Jesus:

> For the Son of man also came not to be served but to serve, and to give his life as a ransom for many (Mk. 10.*45*; see also Mk. 8.*31*; Mt. 8.*20*; Lk. 22.*48*).

Clearly we cannot hope to understand the message and mission of Jesus without reckoning with the creative dynamic of his background and heritage.

### The New Testament presupposes the teaching of the Old Testament

If we had only the New Testament we should find that the revelation of God's nature and purpose afforded us would be incomplete. It is primarily through the Old Testament that we learn of God's work in creation and providence, his attributes of justice, holiness, his power, his glory and wisdom, his word and his spirit. Here, in such a catalogue that could be extended, we see what the New Testament takes for granted about God's personality because he has already shown himself to be like this in his dealings with the Covenant community of Israel. So, too, in the sphere of ethical behaviour and moral standards, the New Testament does not start from scratch but builds on the foundation that has been laid. The Word does become Flesh but this is the great flowering of his purpose, not a magical act of improvisation on God's part.

*The Old and New Testaments are related integrally, as
Promise and Fulfilment*

A recurring phrase in the prophetic writings is 'the days are
coming when':

> Behold, the days are coming, says the Lord, when I will make a new
> covenant with the house of Israel and the house of Judah, not like the
> covenant which I made with their fathers when I took them by the hand
> to bring them out of the land of Egypt, my covenant which they broke,
> though I was their husband, says the Lord . . . I will put my law within
> them, and I will write it upon their hearts; and I will be their God, and
> they shall be my people (Jer. 31.*31-33*; see also Is. 32.*15-17*; 40.*10-11*).

There is always Promise and Fulfilment, from Abraham to
Moses, through the prophets and the psalmists, the same note is
heard that God will keep his promise and fulfil his word. Yet
there is always a characteristic to be noted that these fulfilments
that the Exodus and the Return from Exile represent are both
partial fulfilments only, containing even further promises of what
God is going to do. Rooted as Israel is in her glorious past, she
yet lives by what she looks forward to, by her hopes for the Coming Days. So the comment has been made: 'The future is therefore
the centre of gravity of Israel's faith; the mainspring of her
existence; the source of her vitality, optimism, and hope; the time
of resolution of all the ambiguities and inequalities of the past;
the dawn of a new time' (James Muilenburg, *The Way of Israel*,
p. 129).

The New Testament stands over against these partial fulfilments
of the Old Testament and affirms that God makes his New Covenant with more than a Chosen People, the Hebrews, but with
the whole of mankind. When Jesus says:

> Think not that I have come to abolish the law and the prophets; I have
> come not to abolish them but to fulfil them. For truly, I say to you, till

> heaven and earth pass away, not an iota, not a dot, will pass from the law until all is accomplished (Mt. 5.*17-18*).

this only becomes intelligible when we have experienced what the law and the prophets stand for, and realised afresh that they point beyond to the only adequate fulfilment that the world has known —the Coming of Christ!

Thus, as we begin to consider what the words of the Old Testament mean we are aware that we are not hoping to find rest in a series of propositions but ready to be confronted by a Person, because we shall find a God who Acts!

### FOR FURTHER READING

J. BRIGHT, *The Authority of the Old Testament* (S.C.M., 1967).

R. C. DENTAN, *Preface to Old Testament Theology* (Yale University Press, 1950).

S. MOWINCKEL, *The Old Testament as Word of God* (Blackwell, 1960).

N. W. PORTEOUS, Essay on Old Testament Theology in *The Old Testament and Modern Study* (edited by H. H. Rowley, Oxford, 1951).

J. D. SMART, *The Interpretation of Scripture* (S.C.M., 1961).

PART TWO

# THE REVELATION OF GOD

## 2

## WHAT IS GOD LIKE?
## THE NAMES AND NATURE OF GOD

ONE of the fundamental characteristics of the Hebrew mind is illustrated in the significance that is attached to a person's name. The name is not, as with our Western society, just a label that makes the task of identification easier. The name is looked upon as a kind of description of the owner's personality. A man's name and his nature are indissolubly linked. As with man so with God.

> The Lord bless you and keep you:
>> The Lord make his face to shine upon you, and be gracious to you;
> The Lord lift up his countenance upon you, and give you peace.
> So shall they put my name upon the people of Israel, and I will bless them. (Num. 6.24-27).

The comment in the last verse is significant since we have as parallel 'my name' and 'I'. The use of such parallel terms means to the Hebrew that they may be equated, that is, the name of God stands for God in person. (See below for the discussion of extensions of God's personality, p. 55.)

We then must look closely at the way in which God is described, at what he is called.

## LIVING AND ETERNAL

Again and again we find that the central affirmation of the Old Testament, indeed the whole Bible, is that he is 'the living God'.

### God alive in human history

In the early stories of the struggles of the Hebrews we have a picture of God as a direct participant in their battles, indeed the architect of the nation's victories:

> And Joshua said, 'Hereby you shall know that the living God is among you, and that he will without fail drive out from before you the Canaanites, the Hittites, the Hivites, the Perizzites, the Girgashites, the Amorites, and the Jebusites'. ( Josh. 3.*10*).

The same note is heard in the experience of Isaiah as he describes the siege of Jerusalem by Sennacherib. The Rabshakeh, the Assyrian commander, has contemptuously taunted Hezekiah with the boast that no other gods have ever delivered other nations from the Assyrian might, so why should there be an exception now?

> Who among all the gods of these countries have delivered their countries out of my hand, that the Lord should deliver Jerusalem out of my hand? (Is. 36.*20*).

The prophet assures the king that there is a door that is open, a door of hope.

> It may be that the Lord your God heard the words of the Rabshakeh, whom his master the king of Assyria has sent to mock the living God, and will rebuke the words which the Lord your God has heard; therefore lift up your prayer for the remnant that is left (Is. 37.4).

### God alive in human relationships

From the field of battle we come to the courts of the Temple to meet the living God in the realm of praise and prayer. We hear an exile, who has himself led pilgrims in procession to the sanctuary cry out:

> As a hart longs for flowing streams,
>   so longs my soul for thee, O God.
> My soul thirsts for God,
>   for the living God.
> When shall I come and behold the face of God?
>   My tears have been my food day and night,
>   while men say to me continually,
> 'Where is your God?" (Ps. 42.*1-3*).

Here, beyond the noise of battle, a deeper note is sounded. The living God not only intervenes in history but he shares the living relationship, that is the heart of worship. So a fellow-psalmist exclaims:

> How lovely is thy dwelling place,
>   O Lord of hosts!
> My soul longs, yea, faints for the courts of the Lord;
>   my heart and flesh sing for joy to the living God (Ps. 84.*1-2*).

### God the Source of Life and Eternal

The experience of the Living God gathers momentum. Not only is God alive—he is the source of all life.

> For with thee is the fountain of life;
>   in thy light do we see light (Ps. 36.*9*).

From him comes all the vitality of men and animals and wherever there is life it comes as his gift, although his people did not always acknowledge this:

And she did not know that it was I who gave her the grain, the wine, and
    the oil,
and who lavished upon her silver and gold which they used for Baal
    (Hos. 2.8; Ps. 36.7; Ps. 147.9; Deut. 11.11f.).

So, too, Jeremiah speaks in poignant words:

They have forsaken me,
    the fountain of living waters,
and hewn out cisterns for themselves,
    broken cisterns,
that can hold no water. (Jer. 2.13; see Jn. 4.14).

As the realisation grows that the Israelites indeed have to do
with the Living God it becomes axiomatic that he must be eternal.
So the Psalmists cry out:

Lord, thou has been our dwelling place
    in all generations.
Before the mountains were brought forth,
    or ever thou hadst formed the earth and the world,
from everlasting to everlasting thou art God (Ps. 90.1-2).

Thy eyes beheld my unformed substance;
    in thy book were written every one of them,
the days that were formed for me,
    when as yet there was none of them (Ps. 139.16).

It is important to realise that the emphasis in the Old Testament
is upon the Life of which God is the source and the idea of eternity
is itself derived from that assumption. It has been commented
that God is not living because he is eternal but he is eternal because
he is living. 'The world has a beginning but God has none. There
is no time when He did not exist. The idea that God could have
been born seems absurd to Israel; the Old Testament does not
even argue against it. . . . This silence is one of the strongest
arguments in support of the entirely different nature of Israel's
conception of God, compared with the conceptions of the
neighbouring nations' (T. C. Vriezen, *An Outline of Old Testament Theology*, p. 181).

## ONE AND UNIQUE

Two other qualities of God's nature are brought together in the classical Hebrew affirmation contained in Deut. 6.*4-5*:

> Hear, O Israel: The Lord our God is one Lord; and you shall love the Lord your God with all your heart, and with all your soul, and with all your might. (See also for the use made by Jesus, Mk. 12.*29-30*.)

This passage is called the *Shema*, one of the ancient prayers of the synagogue and incorporated in Jewish liturgy over the centuries up to the present time. The name is derived from the first word which is the Hebrew word for 'Hear'. The essential insistence is upon the unity of God. This is meaningful in the Ancient Near Eastern world where the dominant climate is that of polytheism, the belief in and worship of many gods. God, the Deuteronomic writer is declaring, is not divided as if he were one of a number of the forces of nature, which are frequently thought of as gods in this world, such as the god of the storm, the sun-god, the god of the moon or some other aspect of nature religion. Behind this passage we have the spiritual struggle which is mirrored in the linking of the *Shema* with the demand:

> You shall not go after other gods, of the gods of the peoples who are round about you (Deut. 6.*14*).

The climate of opinion is such that different views of God are growing up in a world that cannot be thought of as a cultural and religious vacuum. There is the need for what many have thought to be the beginning of Hebrew orthodoxy, that is, right ways of thinking about God. Here in the total claim made by God all rivals are eliminated.

This demand for the recognition of the Unity of God is linked inseparably with the belief *in his Uniqueness*. Not only is God One—he alone is God.

We see this belief illustrated in the encounter on Mount Carmel between Elijah and the prophets of Baal. So certain is Elijah that God alone has reality and power that he taunts his opponents:

> Cry aloud, for he is a god; either he is musing, or he has gone aside, or he is on a journey, or perhaps he is asleep and must be awakened (1 Kings 18.27).

The whole point of this is the prophet Elijah's certainty that Yahweh alone is God. God is Unique.

The most impressive witness to this spiritual certainty is found in the writings of Second Isaiah in such passages as:

> Who has directed the Spirit of the Lord,
>     or as his counsellor has instructed him?
> Whom did he consult for his enlightenment,
>     and who taught him the path of justice,
> and taught him knowledge,
>     and showed him the way of understanding? (Is. 40.13-14).

The answer is presupposed—no one because there isn't anyone.

> I am God, and also henceforth I am He;
>     there is none who can deliver from my hand;
> I work and who can hinder it? (Is. 43.13).

This linking of the Unity and Uniqueness of God becomes the source from which Christ himself derives his first and greatest commandment which makes the total demand that only One who is God Alone could make.


### THE NAMES OF GOD

We shall look briefly at three of the most significant names given to God in the Old Testament.

*The name 'God'*

The first name we consider is the word that is translated 'God'. This comes from the Hebrew word, *Elohim*, which is plural in form but there is no question of it having any polytheistic meaning. It is rather a plural of intensity, an expression of the very essence of deity. The name *El* is a general term for 'god' in the Semitic world and especially in Canaanite religion, where El is the supreme, absolute ruler of the gods. The meaning of the word is not universally agreed, but most commentators would support the suggestion that there is an element of power and authority intended when it is used. Some examples will illustrate this:

> Thy steadfast love, O Lord, extends to the heavens,
>    thy faithfulness to the clouds.
> Thy righteousness is like the mountains of God (El),
>    thy judgements are like the great deep (Ps. 36.5-6).
>
> The mountains were covered with its shade,
>    the mighty cedars (of El) with its branches (Ps. 80.10).

In these passages the word El is used to indicate the might and power that is associated with the mountains and cedars and so these characteristics form part of their thinking about God when *El* or *Elohim* is used.

Further support is found for this meaning when we consider the allied term applied to God when he is called *El Shaddai*. So we read in Gen. 17.1:

> When Abram was ninety-nine years old the Lord appeared to Abram, and said to him, 'I am God Almighty; walk before me, and be blameless' (see also Exod. 6.3).

'God Almighty' is the rendering of *El Shaddai*. We know that in Akkadian, the term *sadu* (mountain) is applied to the deities and we can readily see that the strength and stability of the mountain would describe highly desirable qualities of any god. In Hebrew thought we can turn to a striking example of *El Shaddai* being applied to God in Ps. 91:

> He who dwells in the shelter of the Most High,
> who abides in the shadow of the Almighty (El Shaddai) (v.1).

Here the protective strength of God is brought out. The same note is heard in the prophets:

> And when they went, I heard the sound of their wings like the sound of many waters, like the thunder of the Almighty (Shaddai), a sound of tumult like the sound of a host (Ezek. 1.24; see also Is. 13.6).

From these passages we see that *El* and *Elohim* are used to describe the greatness and might of God and especially in the phrase *El Shaddai* do we find the majesty of a mountain god in all his awesome strength and power.


*The name Lord*

The characteristic Israelite name for God is *Yahweh* which is translated 'Lord'. In earliest Hebrew it is expressed by the letters YHWH (called the 'tetragrammaton', meaning four letters). There has been much debate concerning the original meaning of the word and it has been linked with the verb 'to be', or 'to become'. Much more important is the way in which the name is used and what it meant for the Hebrew writers. Two passages will give us some indication of the significance of the name and so the nature of Yahweh: our first passage is found in the Song of Deborah which is a major source for early thought and belief. We read of Yahweh and his deeds:

> Lord (Yahweh), when thou didst go forth from Seir,
> when thou didst march from the region of Edom,

the earth trembled, and the heavens dropped,
  yea, the clouds dropped water.
The mountains quaked before the Lord (Yahweh),
  yon Sinai before the Lord (Yahweh), the God (Elohim) of Israel
  (Judg. 5.4-5).

My heart goes out to the commanders of Israel
  who offered themselves willingly among the people.
Bless the Lord (Yahweh).

To the sound of musicians at the watering places,
  there they repeat the triumphs of the Lord (Yahweh),
the triumphs of his peasantry in Israel (Judg. 5.9,11).

Clearly, belief in Yahweh means belief in his power in heaven and on earth. He is the embodiment of power and is capable of bringing forth a response from his people Israel.

The second major passage for understanding something of what Yahweh meant is found in Exodus:

Then Moses said to God, 'If I come to the people of Israel, and say to them, "The God of your fathers has sent me to you," and they ask me, "What is his name?" what shall I say to them?' God said to Moses, 'I AM WHO I AM.' And he said, 'Say this to the people of Israel, "I AM has sent me to you." ' (Ex. 3.13-14).

The passage ostensibly gives an explanation of the derivation of the name Yahweh and connects it with the verb 'to be'. Yet whatever the view held about the original root employed, there is no escaping the fact that the passage with the description of the Burning Bush and God's revelation of his name Yahweh has two main affirmations at its heart. First, that God was a holy God to be approached with awe and secondly, that this same God was personally with his people and would deliver them from their bondage in Egypt. The Hebrews never forgot that it was Yahweh, their God, who said:

I am Yahweh your God, who brought you out of the land of Egypt, out of the house of bondage (Ex. 20.2).

It was this experience that seared Hebrew imagination and the name Yahweh continued to have the significance of the Living God who was ever-present with his people to deliver them as he had delivered their fathers. Yahweh was their Covenant God.

### The Lord of Hosts

A third name given to God and one which occurs especially frequently in the prophetic writings is that of 'the Lord of Hosts' and sometimes in the fuller form 'the Lord God of Hosts'.

> Of the increase of his government and of peace
>     there will be no end,
> upon the throne of David, and over his kingdom,
>     to establish it, and to uphold it
> with justice and with righteousness
>     from this time forth and for evermore.
> The zeal of the Lord of hosts will do this (Is. 9.7; see also Hos. 12.5;
>     Amos 3.13).

Three main suggestions have been made as to the meaning of this title given to God. It might refer to the earthly forces of the Israelite armies or the hosts of the heavenly bodies, the sun, moon and stars, or even the spirits that might be thought to reside in the celestial bodies. A recent comment has been, 'the prophets saw in the use of the expression a polemical point directed against the spread of the cult of the stars which were thought to animate them, and in the face of which it had to be affirmed that Yahweh was the only lord of the army of the heavens' (Jacob, *Theology of the Old Testament*, p. 55).

The underlying affirmation is that the Lordship of God is total—there is One God! We see that to call God by his names is a significant activity—it is to proclaim one's Credo.

## YAHWEH AND OTHER GODS

As far as Ancient Israel is concerned it is soon clear that the God who is alive and active in history and human experience is the supreme God. They had long realised that as Israel had Yahweh so the people of Moab had Chemosh and the people of Ammon had Melek. Yet the question must be asked—is Yahweh just one of the others? Is he greater than they are or inferior? The Old Testament had no doubt about the answer. Some of the following passages give the evidence. We have in God's covenant with Abraham the implicit claim of the Lordship of all the nations in:

> I will bless those who bless you, and him who curses you I will curse; and by you all the families of the earth will bless themselves (Gen. 12.3).

And again in Abraham's remonstrating with God himself to act like God, we read:

> Far be that from thee! Shall not the Judge of all the earth do right? (Gen. 18.25).

In the prophets we early have the belief that there is no other god who has power over human lives:

> Did I not bring up Israel from the land of Egypt,
>     and the Philistines from Caphtor
> and the Syrians from Kir? (Amos 9.7; see also Jer. 2.5,11).

It was Second Isaiah who drew out the ultimate consequences of having faith in the One, Living, Unique God. This he does through such a passage as his picture painted in scathing terms of an idol factory in Babylon, with men gathered around their end-product:

> Everyone helps his neighbour,
>     and says to his brother, 'Take courage!'

The craftsman encourages the goldsmith,
  and he who smooths with the hammer him who strikes the anvil,
  saying of the soldering, 'It is good';
and they fasten it with nails so that it cannot be moved (Is. 41.6-7; see also
  40.*18-20*; 44.*12-17*).

This is the contrast between the living and the dead. In more positive fashion, the prophet affirms:

Declare and present your case;
  let them take counsel together!
Who told this long ago?
  Who declared it of old?
Was it not I, the Lord?
  And there is no other god besides me,
a righteous God and a Saviour;
  there is none besides me (Is. 45.*21*; 43.*9*; 44.*6*).

The other gods are not merely inferior and powerless, they are nonentities, they do not even exist.

In a final passage from the closing book in the Old Testament we have a rebuke of the superficiality of much of what passed for worship in Malachi's day, a time of spiritual tiredness:

Oh, that there were one among you who would shut the doors, that you might not kindle fire upon my altar in vain! I have no pleasure in you, says the Lord of hosts, and I will not accept an offering from your hand. For from the rising of the sun to its setting my name is great among the nations, and in every place incense is offered to my name, and a pure offering; for my name is great among the nations, says the Lord of hosts (Mal. 1.*10-11*).

The spiritual audacity is breathtaking—although the members of the other Gentile nations may think they are worshipping their own gods—in reality they are worshipping the God Almighty, the Lord of hosts!

## FOR FURTHER READING

E. JACOB, *Old Testament Theology* (Hodder & Stoughton, 1958).
L. KOEHLER, *Old Testament Theology* (Lutterworth, 1957).
H. RINGGREN, *Israelite Religion* (S.P.C.K., 1966).
T. C. VRIEZEN, *An Outline of Old Testament Theology* (Blackwell, 1958).
T. C. VRIEZEN, *The Religion of Ancient Israel* (Lutterworth, 1967).

# 3

# WHAT DOES GOD DO?
# THE GOD WHO ACTS

FROM our examination of the nature of God and the significance of the names given to him, it might have seemed a logical next step to ask what is God like, what are his attributes? Yet this would be the wrong way to go about it. We must first ask the question which heads this section—what does God do? It is in the light of what God does that we shall see more clearly what he is like. His actions are the best key to his attributes. We shall find out what sort of God he is when we have reckoned with what he has done for us.

### GOD AS REDEEMER

It might seem strange that we do not look first at God as Creator. Yet strangely enough the Hebrew writers did not regard creation as the primary act of God but rather saw creation as part of God's plan to redeem the world. So it has been well said: 'To the question Why has God created the world? the Old Testament would answer: He has created it for the covenant, that is to say, because of his plan of love and salvation for humanity by means of Israel, in creating the world God already had the

covenant in view and it is this motive which gave to the idea
of creation its specific orientation' (E. Jacob, *Theology of the Old
Testament*, p. 137).

The order of their spiritual experience is: first their awareness
of God as Redeemer and Saviour and then, with this consciousness
in mind, who else could be their Creator?

### The significance of Redemption

There are two main words used to describe this act of God—
that of redeeming his people. The first is *padah* which is used of
ransoming a person or living thing by giving an equivalent.
This word says nothing about the status of the one who redeems.
The other word is *go'el* (redeemer) and it is used of one who
belongs to the family circle. He is the next of kin who assumes the
duties and privileges of the nearest relative. He must stand by his
poor relation who may have lost his property or become enslaved
or suffered bereavement. When God is spoken of as a redeemer
it is always from within the circle of the family he has himself
created. (See Lev. 25.*23*; Ruth 3.*12-13*.)

Some passages will illustrate the ways in which these terms are
used to describe God as a redeemer:

> But it is because the Lord loves you, and is keeping the oath which he
> swore to your fathers, that the Lord has brought you out with a mighty
> hand, and *redeemed* you from the house of bondage, from the hand of
> Pharaoh, king of Egypt (Deut. 7.*8*).

> For I know that my *Redeemer* lives,
>     and at last he will stand upon the earth (Job 19.*25*).

Especially significant is the close link between Creation and
Redeemer when we look at the teaching of Second Isaiah (chs.
40–55) where repeatedly the prophet speaks of God as the Holy
One, the Redeemer of Israel:

Thus says the Lord,
the Redeemer of Israel and his Holy One,
to one deeply despised, abhorred by the nations,
the servant of rulers:
'Kings shall see and arise;
princes, and they shall prostrate themselves;
because of the Lord, who is faithful,
the Holy One of Israel, who has chosen you' (Is. 49.7).

But now thus says the Lord, he who created you, O Jacob, he who formed
you O Israel:
'Fear not, for I have redeemed you;
I have called you by name, you are mine' (Is. 43.1; see also 43.7,15;
44.2,21).

The prophet is thinking about God's action at two creative moments: the creation of an ordered world out of a watery chaos and the deliverance from Egypt. The day of deliverance that lies in the future is an act of creation just as much as the first act of creation. This is the climax of all redeeming, that man becomes a new creation so that God can say again you are mine! To redeem is to recreate.

There is, however, a major difference between a man redeeming a near relative and God redeeming his people, that cannot be over-emphasised. This concerns the payment of a redemption price, a ransom. The essential point is that God the Sovereign Lord of all creation redeems his people through grace—he gives no equivalent when he redeems. He is not involved in a legal process when he expresses his redeeming purpose, but in the continuation of his creation. Creation needs a redeeming before it is complete.

## GOD AS SAVIOUR

There are three points of emphasis in the Old Testament idea of Salvation.

*Salvation means victory*

In early contexts salvation means victory. So in Judges 15.*16,18*
we read of Samson's victory over the Philistines:

> 'With the jawbone of an ass have I slain a thousand men' . . . and he was
> very thirsty, and he called on the Lord and said 'Thou hast granted this
> great deliverance by the hand of thy servant' [the word 'deliverance' is
> actually 'salvation'].

Similarly, Jonathan is given the victory against the Philistines
at Michmash.

> And Jonathan said to the young man who bore his armour, 'Come, let
> us go over to the garrison of these uncircumcised; it may be that the Lord
> will work for us; for nothing can hinder the Lord from saving by many or
> by few' (1 Sam. 14.*6*).

*Salvation is positive*

Not only does God save *from* but he saves *for*—the extension of
his purpose. A good example of the positive side of salvation is
found in the well-loved 91st Psalm. Here we have a picture of the
power of God. Demonic forces may rage against the psalmist
and plagues may surround him yet he is able to end his psalm with
God in his own person speaking:

> Because he cleaves to me in love, I will deliver him;
> I will protect him, because he knows my name.
> When he calls to me I will answer him;
> I will be with him in trouble,
> I will rescue him and honour him
> With long life I will satisfy him,
> and show him my salvation (Ps. 91.*14-16*).

The whole song is summed up in the last word—Salvation.
The person who commits his life to God shall find his every
purpose included and taken up into God's salvation.

*Salvation yesterday, today and tomorrow*

A further characteristic of what the Old Testament means by saying God is a Saviour is that his saving acts are affirmed of the past, the present and the future. Of the past certainly but also the present reality is affirmed:

> Not with our fathers did the Lord make this covenant, but with us, who are all of us here alive this day (Deut. 5.3).

The four-fold emphasis on the present is clear—with us, who are all of us here, alive, this day. Each successive phrase sounds the same note and reinforces it. Yet in a time of tension and longing for the coming Messiah, Zechariah is able to affirm, when the spiritual climate is one of lethargy and half-hearted attempt to rebuild a ruined world, that God will act and again in his own words:

> Behold, I will save my people from the east country and from the west country, and I will bring them to dwell in the midst of Jerusalem; and they shall be my people and I will be their God, in faithfulness and in righteousness (Zech. 8.7-8).

His people may be scattered throughout the world but God will provide them with living room—with salvation!

## GOD AS CREATOR

It is against the background of God as Redeemer and Saviour that we can now best understand what the Old Testament says about God the Creator because we can readily grasp that Creation to the Hebrew mind cannot be seen as an arbitrary act of power but the expression of God's purpose to redeem and save the world. It is significant that the first verse of Genesis commences: 'In the beginning God created the heavens and the earth' (Gen. 1.1).

The word translated 'beginning' means much more than a time-marker. Genesis represents the beginning of a plan of action that springs from God's purpose to bring about a relationship between himself and the man he is going to create. It is not without significance that the only subject of the verb translated 'create' is God himself. The object of this verb is never a substance, a raw material or something half completed, but always the perfected work.

### Creation through God's Word

When we consider what the Bible says about the instruments or agents of God's creative power, we see first the significance of his Creative Word. Immediately in the first chapter of Genesis we find the phrase 'And God said' used creatively eight times (vv. 3, 6, 9, 11, 14, 20, 24 and 26).

The idea of a creative word or fiat is known elsewhere in the Ancient Near East but the significance of the word of God is related to what the god is like and the belief in the One Universal God gives a meaning to his creative word that is not paralleled elsewhere.

Two passages will illustrate this belief in the creative power of God's Word; one is taken from the prophets and one from the psalms.

> For as the rain and the snow come down from heaven,
>     and return not thither but water the earth,
> making it bring forth and sprout,
>     giving seed to the sower and bread to the eater,
> so shall my word be that goes forth from my mouth;
>     it shall not return to me empty,
> but it shall accomplish that which I purpose,
>     and prosper in the thing for which I sent it (Is. 55.10-11).

The word of God of which the prophet speaks is clearly more than a verbal utterance. It has a dynamic creative power.

So the psalmist bears his testimony too:

> By the word of the Lord the heavens were made,
>   and all their host by the breath of his mouth. . . .
> For he spoke, and it came to be;
>   he commanded, and it stood forth (Ps. 33.6-9).

### Creation through God's Spirit

A second instrument of God's creative power as portrayed in the Old Testament is his Creative Spirit. A close link exists between Spirit and Word in Hebrew thought and these two agents used by God in creation are not to be thought of as opposed. The Hebrew word for spirit is the same as that used for wind, i.e. air in motion, and the utterance of a word involves this movement of air in the form of breath through the mouth. So often we find the two ideas used as parallels.

> The Lord also thundered in the heavens,
>   and the Most High uttered his voice,
> hailstones and coals of fire.

> And he sent out his arrows, and scattered them;
> he flashed forth lightnings, and routed them.
>   Then the channels of the sea were seen,
> and the foundations of the world were laid bare,
>   at thy rebuke, O Lord,
> at the blast of the *breath* of thy nostrils (Ps. 18.13-15).

Again the description of the liberation of the Exodus, the event that created the Hebrew nation is described as due to Yahweh's intervention in the form of a dynamic wind:

> Then Moses stretched out his hand over the sea; and the Lord drove the sea back by a strong east wind all night, and made the sea dry land (Exod. 14.21, see Exod. 15.8 too, which reads:

At the blast of thy nostrils the waters piled up,
the floods stood up in a heap).

In particular the creative power of the Spirit is affirmed in
Psalm 104.*29-30*:

When thou hidest thy face, they are dismayed;
when thou takest away their breath, they die
and return to their dust.
When thou sendest forth thy Spirit, they are created;
and thou renewest the face of the ground.

## Creation through God's Wisdom

As well as creation through his Word and Spirit, in the later
writings called the Wisdom literature (discussed in Vol. I of this
series: see H. Mowvley, *The Testimony of Israel*, ch. 11) we have a
number of passages that speak of God's Wisdom in the same way
as Word and Spirit:

The Lord by wisdom founded the earth;
by understanding he established the heavens;
by his knowledge the deeps broke forth,
and the clouds drop down the dew (Prov. 3.*19-20*).

In another passage Wisdom speaks as a person:

When he established the heavens, I was there,
when he drew a circle on the face of the deep,
when he made firm the skies above,
when he established the fountains of the deep
when he assigned to the sea its limit,
so that the waters might not transgress his command,
when he marked out the foundations of the earth,
then I was beside him, like a master workman (Prov. 8.*27-30*; see also
Job 28 and Wisdom of Solomon 1.*6-7*; 7.*22f.*).

The debate still continues as to what the poet means in this last
passage but many have seen much more than a mere personifica-
tion and in a number of passages elsewhere we approach the

meaning of a being or person who stands for and represents God in his creative role. The clear linking of Wisdom with Word and Spirit suggests that we have in all three cases an extension of divine personality. That is, to speak of God's Word, his Spirit and his Wisdom is the same as speaking of God himself. (See specially, A. R. Johnson, *The One and the Many in the Israelite Conception of God*, pp. 18–21.)

### GOD AS PROVIDENCE

We have seen that God as Creator is clearly linked with God as Redeemer. It is the experience of being redeemed by God that led to the certainty of the affirmation that He and He alone could be the Creator. A further aspect of God's activity must be mentioned, that is, his Providence. It is not enough to say that God created the world but he keeps his world in existence and uses it to express his purpose because he still governs and directs it. His providence is this continuing creative action of God. There is no place for belief in other gods and quite certainly no room for any modern concept of chance. He initiates all and sustains and maintains all. Through his spirit both man and animals live and when life ends, this spirit or breath of life returns to him. Ecclesiastes in moving terms describes such a return of the spirit that maintains all life to its source:

> Because man goes to his eternal home, and mourners go about the streets; before the silver cord is snapped, or the golden bowl is broken, or the pitcher is broken at the fountain, or the wheel broken at the cistern, and the dust returns to the earth as it was, and the spirit returns to God who gave it (Eccles. 12.5-7).

The Psalmists specially praise God for his providence in making provision for the continuation of life for animals, mankind, the world of Nature:

Thy righteousness is like the mountains of God,
   thy judgements are like the great deep;
man and beast thou savest, O Lord (Ps. 36.6).

He covers the heavens with clouds,
   he prepares rain for the earth,
he makes grass grow upon the hills.
   He gives to the beasts their food,
and to the young ravens which cry (Ps. 147.8-9).

What of the experience of misfortune and sorrow? These, too, come within the divine providence. So prophets and psalmists agree:

Does evil befall a city, unless the Lord has done it? (Amos 3.6).

I form light and create darkness,
   I make weal and create woe,
I am the Lord, who do all these things (Is. 45.7).

Whatever the harshness of life with its bitterness and resentments at its injustice and inequalities yet the psalmist by God's providence can yet say:

When my soul was embittered,
   when I was pricked in heart,
I was stupid and ignorant,
   I was like a beast toward thee.
Nevertheless I am continually with thee. . . .
   My flesh and my heart may fail,
but God is the strength of my heart and my portion for ever (Ps.
   73.21-26).

Such a sense of God's guiding providence fully illustrates a perceptive comment: 'He is the Creator; that means distance; He is also the Maintainer, and that means communion' (T. C. Vriezen, *An Outline of Old Testament Theology*, p. 191).

## GOD AS LORD OF HISTORY

History has been called the sacrament of the religion of Israel. Certainly there is an indissoluble link between Israel's faith and her history. A striking example of how Hebrew faith is rooted in the events of history is seen in the most ancient confession of faith:

> And you shall make response before the Lord your God, 'A wandering Aramean was my father; and he went down into Egypt and sojourned there, few in number; and there he became a nation, great, mighty, and populous. And the Egyptians treated us harshly, and afflicted us, and laid upon us hard bondage . . . . And the Lord brought us out of Egypt with a mighty hand and an outstretched arm . . . and he brought us into this place and gave us this land, a land flowing with milk and honey (Deut. 26.5; see also Josh. 24.3-6).

It is highly significant that there is a complete absence of any theoretical comment about God. Here is affirmation—He is active in history here and now!

Other examples of God using history as his arena or workshop are found in the way that he guides the fortunes of Abraham (Gen. 22) and Joseph:

> As for you, you meant evil against me; but God meant it for good, to bring it about that many people should be kept alive as they are today (Gen. 50.20).

God's over-riding purpose in history includes that of other nations beyond Israel's border. So God speaks to Cyrus, Persian conqueror:

> Thus says the Lord to his anointed, to Cyrus whose right hand I have grasped,
> to subdue nations before him to ungird the loins of kings. . . .
> I gird you, though you do not know me (Is. 45.1,5; see also Amos 9.7).

God is the initiator of all history and his lordship includes all nations and all ages until its consummation.

> For behold, I create new heavens
>   and a new earth;
> and the former things shall not be remembered
>   or come into mind.
> But be glad and rejoice for ever
>   in that which I create (Is. 65.17-18).

## FOR FURTHER READING

W. EICHRODT, *Theology of the Old Testament* (II, S.C.M., 1967).

A. R. JOHNSON, *The One and the Many in the Israelite Conception of God* (Univ. of Wales Press, 1942, 2nd ed. 1961).

G. E. WRIGHT, *The God Who Acts* (S.C.M., 1952).

# 4

## WHAT IS GOD LIKE?
## THE ATTRIBUTES OF GOD

OUR next question follows directly after our finding some answers to the former one—what does God do? It is essential that we retain this order. We can only say what God is like when we realise the nature of what he does. His attributes are to be discerned in his actions. Having seen the dominant emphasis in the Old Testament is always upon the fact that God acts there is still place for a brief examination of what, in the light of what he so triumphantly does, the Bible writers say about his attributes.

### GOD IN HUMAN TERMS

Our starting-point must be the fact that when God is described it is always in terms and expressions that are used of human feelings and emotions, of relationships that are a natural part of human society and family. The technical term for this describing God in terms that are applicable to man is 'anthropomorphism' (in form of man) from the Greek, *anthropos*—man, and *morphe*—form or shape. So we read of God speaking in the very act of creation (Gen. 1.*3, 6, 9, 11, 14, 20, 24, 26*) and walking in the garden and conversing with Adam, which presupposes hearing and sight

(Gen. *3.8-11*) while after the waters of the flood had subsided and Noah offers his sacrifice to God we read that God 'smelled the pleasing odour' (Gen. 8.*21*). Similarly God is described as laughing (Ps. 2.*4*) and whistling (Is. 7.*18*). In addition to these human faculties attributed to God so too he thinks and feels like a human being. So he rejoices with joy (Zeph. 3.*17*), is disgusted (Is. 1.*13*), repents (Gen. 6.*6*) and is jealous (Ex. 20.*5*).

Two further comments are necessary to see this characteristic feature of the Old Testament way of describing God as a man, in the true perspective.

### First, it represents a profound insight, not a primitive throw-back

The deepest moment of a man's spiritual experience must be described in human terms of his own experience of other men and women. He has no other experience or language and when Hosea describes God as a lover (*2.14-20*) or a father (11.*1-4*) here is no cheap loose way of speaking but the use of the dearest human terms to describe how he believed God felt about his people. To dismiss such human terms as primitive becomes blasphemy.

### Secondly, there is in the Old Testament a recognition that God is greater than all human description

As far as speech will allow human functions and feelings are used of God but never with any sense that the Living God is now neatly defined—and destroyed! So we read in the prophets especially:

> For I am God and not man,
>     the Holy One in your midst,
> and I will not come to destroy (Hos. 11.*9*).

and again:

> For my thoughts are not your thoughts, neither are your ways my
> ways, says the Lord. For as the heavens are higher than the earth, so are
> my ways higher than your ways and my thoughts than your thoughts
> (Is. 55.*8-9*).

When God meets man face to face there is never any danger of
man becoming 'too pally with the Almighty' just because God
is described in human terms. He is so described but he is never
limited by or behind such language. Rather than seeing this as a
defect we should rejoice that the O.T. writers were so over-
whelmed by the sense of the living God that they so described
him and, most significantly, from such a starting-point we are
embarked upon a pilgrimage that will bring us to the Incarnation
—God made Flesh! (Jn. 1.*14*).

### GOD AS HOLY

The description of God as holy is illustrated notably in two
familiar Bible scenes. The first is the Call Vision of Isaiah:

> In the year that King Uzziah died I saw the Lord sitting upon a throne,
> high and lifted up; and his train filled the temple. Above him stood the
> seraphim; each had six wings: with two he covered his face, and with two
> he covered his feet, and with two he flew. And one called to another and
> said:
>   Holy, holy, holy is the Lord of hosts;
>     the whole earth is full of his glory (6.*1-3*).

Confronted by this Holy God we are not surprised that Isaiah's
reaction should be:

> Woe is me! For I am lost; for I am a man of unclean lips, and I dwell in
> the midst of a people of unclean lips; for my eyes have seen the King,
> the Lord of hosts! (6.*5*).

The second is at the mountain of God, Horeb, where God

commissions Moses in the encounter that leads to the birth of the Israelite nation. The action is described:

> And the angel of the Lord appeared to him in a flame of fire out of the midst of a bush; and he looked, and lo, the bush was burning, yet it was not consumed. And Moses said, 'I will turn aside and see this great sight, why the bush is not burnt'. When the Lord saw that he turned aside to see, God called to him out of the bush 'Moses, Moses!' And he said, 'Here am I'. Then he said, 'Do not come near; put off your shoes from your feet, for the place on which you are standing is holy ground' (Ex. 3.2-5).

Holiness is, however, much more than one among a series of qualities; it is essentially what being God is about, it corresponds to his deity. The basic meaning of the word is disputed, since two main ideas are put forward. The first is that it comes from a root meaning to cut or separate, while an alternative view is that it is derived from a root meaning to shine, to be brilliant. Yet its original derivation does not exhaust the meaning of the term when actually used.

The essential usage may be illustrated as we consider three characteristics of the idea of holiness.

### Holiness as Separation from and Separation for

In the Old Testament we find that holy persons and objects are those that are separated from ordinary, everyday usage and dedicated to the service of God. When the Old Testament speaks of a holy mountain, a holy city or a holy people (Is. 11.9; Joel 3.17; Deut. 7.6) the central idea is that the mountain or city or people are the personal possession of God and are set apart for his service. They belong completely to God. God is the source of all that is holy and he is other than man.

> I will not execute my fierce anger,
> I will not again destroy Ephraim;

> for I am God and not man,
>   the Holy One in your midst,
>   and I will not come to destroy (Hos. 11.*9*).

That God is separate from man is another way of saying that he is other than man, that is, holy.

### Holiness means a Relationship

The Old Testament knows nothing about self-contained holiness. The Holy God is always pictured as being in the midst of his people who, because they are God's possession, must also partake of his nature. The holiness of God is communicated to men and in some cases it is thought of as a physical contagion that could be transmitted. Two passages illustrate these emphases. The first is the incident of Uzzah who touches the holy Ark of God and is infected.

> And the anger of the Lord was kindled against Uzzah; and God smote him there because he put forth his hand to the ark (2 Sam. 6.7).

A second passage underlines the communication of holiness from God to his people.

> And the Lord said to Moses, 'Say to all the congregation of the people of Israel, You shall be holy; for I the Lord your God am holy' (Lev. 19.2; 21.*8*; 22.*9,31*).

### The Holy God Redeems

We have seen already that one of the great acts of God, even the supreme purpose he has, is the redeeming of man. Here we add an additional note, that is, the relationship between the Holy God and the Redeemer. In a number of passages the link is shown to be integral. It is because God is Holy that he Redeems—he must communicate his own nature. So we read in Second Isaiah:

Thus says the Lord,
  your Redeemer, the Holy One of Israel:
'For your sake I will send to Babylon
  and break down all the bars,
and the shouting of the Chaldeans will be turned to lamentations' (Is.
  43.*14*).

Our Redeemer—the Lord of hosts is his name—
  is the Holy One of Israel (Is. 47.*4*).

Thus says the Lord,
  your Redeemer, the Holy One of Israel:
'I am the Lord your God,
  who teaches you to profit,
who leads you in the way you should go' (Is. 48.*17*; see also 49.7; 43.*3*).


## GOD AS RIGHTEOUS

The fundamental idea behind the Hebrew word that is translated 'righteous' is that of correspondence to a standard or norm.
That is, the very opposite of being arbitrary or capricious, frequent
attributes of deity in the Ancient Near East. For example, in the
familiar and much-loved 23rd Psalm, the phrase 'paths of
righteousness' means paths that are straight not crooked. From a
physical norm the thought behind 'righteous' is applied to a
moral standard and so we have a frequent link between the
righteousness and justice of God (Ps. 98.*9*).

Two features of God's righteousness must be mentioned.


### Righteousness and Justice

The idea of the righteous God cannot be separated from God
the judge. This is seen admirably expressed in the account of
Abraham's intercession on behalf of Sodom in which he actually
pleads with God to act like a God!

> Far be it from thee to do such a thing, to slay the righteous with the wicked, so that the righteous fare as the wicked! Far be that from thee! Shall not the Judge of all the earth do right? (Gen. 18.25).

This means that Abraham is reminding God of his own nature. He must be just because this is his nature or norm, because he is a righteous God! So too when the prophet Amos thunders forth:

> But let justice roll down like waters,
>     and righteousness like an ever flowing stream (5.24; see also 7.7,8).

The judgement holds good that 'this is a Copernican revolution in man's thinking about God. He is not arbitrary, wilful and despotic but righteous and just' (E. Jones, *Profiles of the Prophets*, p. 24).

### Righteousness and Grace

In contrast to our later Western ideas about justice and righteousness that tend to acquire a hard legalistic emphasis, the biblical concept of the righteous God is not of this impartial kind. 'The justice of Yahweh is not of the type of the blindfolded maiden holding a balance in her hand; the justice of Yahweh extends one arm to the wretch stretched out on the ground whilst the other pushes away the one who causes the misfortunes' (Jacob, *Theology of the Old Testament*, p. 99).

The righteous God is one who because he is righteous (as this is his nature or norm) is ever seeking to deliver the one who has failed, not always on the look out to pounce on any human error.

Two passages especially underline this integral link between God the Judge and the God who saves. In Second Isaiah the prophet affirms as he taunts the idol maker of Babylon:

> Declare and present your case;
>     let them take counsel together!

> Who told this long ago?
>   Who declared it of old?
> Was it not I, the Lord?
>   And there is no other god besides me,
> a righteous God and a Saviour (Is. 45.*21*).

Sometimes this has been misunderstood. There is no tension between differing parts of God's nature, as if a perpetual tug-of-war was going on inside him! He would like to save men but he can't because he is a righteous God! It is precisely because he is righteous that he will save. The righteous God is the God who communicates his righteousness to the sinner and justifies him, that is 'puts him in the right'. This because of his own nature. So Hosea speaks of the gifts of a loving husband to his erring wife after she has returned to the family she had left:

> And I will betroth you to me in righteousness and in justice, in steadfast love, and in mercy. I will betroth you to me in faithfulness; and you shall know the Lord (Hos. 2.*19-20*).

## GOD AS FAITHFUL

Our last-quoted passage of scripture uses a number of terms that describe the actions and so the attributes of God. Specifically we want to comment on two that are frequently found in parallel lines, that is, with a significance that is synonymous. They are 'steadfast love' and 'faithfulness'. This close association is found in such passages from the Psalms:

> All the paths of the Lord are steadfast love and faithfulness,
>   for those who keep his covenant and his testimonies (Ps. 25.*10*).

And again:

> I have not hid thy saving help within my heart,
>   I have spoken of thy faithfulness and thy salvation:
> I have not concealed thy steadfast love and thy faithfulness
>   from the great congregation (Ps. 40.*10*).

The word translated 'steadfast love' has been variously rendered as 'faithfulness, devotion, loving-kindness, leal-love or troth'. These are attempts to bring out the element of strength and stability. The steadfast love or covenant love of God is not an emotional feeling, subjective and fleeting, but it has a strong resolute inner core of stability. This is a recurring note of the Old Testament. God is not fickle, he can be trusted.

Of particular interest is a recent translation of a verse in Isaiah:

> So that he who blesses himself in the land
>   shall bless himself by the God of the Amen,
> and he who takes an oath in the land
>   shall swear by the God of the Amen (Is. 65.*16*).

The R.S.V. reads 'God of truth' but the original is the root from which 'Amen' comes, and carries the idea of stability and trustworthiness; so when we read the comment, 'He may even be called the *God of the Amen*' (T. C. Vriezen, *An Outline of Old Testament Theology*, pp. 160–161), we understand what they are saying about God. He is faithful, stable, and true. The undertones are not those of an intellectual grasp of truth but the lasting relationship of God with man, which he initiated and which he sustains. So in the account of the covenant which God made on Sinai with Moses the opening testimony reads:

> The Lord, the Lord, a God merciful and gracious, slow to anger, and abounding in steadfast love and faithfulness (Ex. 34.*6*).

It is this certainty that God is faithful that causes another Hebrew centuries later to bear his witness:

> As surely as God is faithful, our word to you has not been Yes and No. . . . For all the promises of God find their Yes in him. That is why we utter the Amen through him, to the glory of God (2 Cor. 1.*18,20*).

## FOR FURTHER READING

G. A. F. KNIGHT, *A Christian Theology of the Old Testament* (S.C.M., 1959).
L. KOEHLER, *Old Testament Theology* (Lutterworth, 1957).
N. H. SNAITH, *The Distinctive Ideas of the Old Testament* (Epworth, 1944).
T. C. VRIEZEN, *An Outline of Old Testament Theology* (Blackwell, 1958).

# 5

## HOW GOD SHOWS HIMSELF

ONE of the dominant notes of the Old Testament is that of Revelation. This is much nearer the heart of the Bible than any idea of man searching for God and discovering him and his purpose through renewed and dedicated application to his quest. The whole of the Bible story emphasises that God takes the initiative and man responds—it is God who shows himself rather than man who discovers God!

This is the force of the irony of God's speech to Job:

> Where were you when I laid the foundation of the earth?
>> Tell me, if you have understanding,
> Who determined its measurements
>> —surely you know! (Job 38.4-5).

Again and again man has echoed the plea of Job:

> Oh, that I knew where I might find him,
>> that I might come even to his seat! (Job 23.3).

The Bible answers that this is only possible if God makes himself known, and so he assuredly does. The whole of the Bible could rightly be summarised as God's Revelation and Man's Response.

We shall now seek to make good this judgement by looking more closely at the various ways in which God does this.

## GOD REVEALS HIMSELF THROUGH NATURE

Although quite familiar with the deification of natural pro-
cesses found in the Ancient Near Eastern religions, such as
looking upon the Sun and the Moon, the Storm and Rain as
gods, the Hebrew mind had the audacity to reject the identification of God with the world that he had made. God is the Lord
of Nature but Nature is never God.

To illustrate God's self-revelation in the world of nature we
may examine Psalm 8.

> O Lord, our Lord,
> How majestic is thy name in all the earth!
>
> .        .        .        .        .        .        .        .
>
> When I look at thy heavens, the work of thy fingers,
> the moon and the stars which thou hast established;
> what is man that thou art mindful of him,
> and the son of man that thou dost care for him? (vv.*1, 3-4*).

The psalmist describes how he feels when he contemplates
the splendour of the heavens. Yet what overwhelms him is not so
much the sublime beauty of the sky at night, but the realisation
that it is his God who is behind it all. As the sky stretches over all
the earth so does God's glory embrace heaven and earth. In v.*4*
we reach the heart of the psalm:

> What is man that thou art mindful of him,
> and the son of man that thou dost care for him?

These words are often heard in the context of biological,
sociological or psychological questionings. But this is to distort
the psalmist's meaning. The psalmist is affirming God's majesty
as seen in the world of nature, but certainly God is not to be
equated with any natural force. The sun, moon and stars reveal
him and obey him but they are not thought of as deities.

A further passage from the psalms underlines the relationship between God and Nature:

> Bless the Lord, O my soul!
>   O Lord my God, thou art very great!
> Thou art clothed with honour and majesty,
>   who coverest thyself with light as with a garment,
> who hast stretched out the heavens like a tent,
>   who hast laid the beams of thy chambers on the waters,
> who makest the clouds thy chariot,
>   who ridest on the wings of the wind,
> who makest the winds thy messengers,
>   fire and flame thy ministers (Ps. 104.1-4).

The psalmist, after describing the wonders of the world of Nature created by God, continues with an account of the way that God sustains it:

> When thou hidest thy face, they are dismayed;
>   when thou takest away their breath, they die
> and return to their dust (Ps. 104.29).

In God, the whole of creation, the world of nature and mankind all have their beginning and ending. Through the process of Nature, God continued his act of creation.

## GOD REVEALS HIMSELF THROUGH HISTORY

In the events of both national and individual life, the Hebrews had no doubt that the Living God acted. History, for them, was the history of salvation. The Old Testament knows nothing of a God who is merely existent. They only believe in his existence because they have experienced what he has done. In history he has his workshop, it is the sphere where he reveals his purpose— to create a covenant relationship between himself and mankind. An outstanding example of God's revelation of himself in the events of history is seen in Psalm 105. (See also Pss. 78, 106 and

114.) In this psalm we see history as the sphere where he works out his covenant purpose.

The opening verses (*1–6*) suggest a festival occasion where pilgrims have gathered to remember and recount the saving deeds of God.

> Remember the wonderful works that he has done,
>     his miracles, and the judgments he uttered,
> O offspring of Abraham his servant,
>     sons of Jacob, his chosen ones! (vv. *5-6*).

> He is mindful of his covenant for ever,
>     of the word that he commanded, for a thousand generations,
> the covenant which he made with Abraham,
>     his sworn promise to Isaac,
> which he confirmed to Jacob . . . as an everlasting covenant,
>     saying, 'To you I will give the land of Canaan
> as your portion for an inheritance' (vv. *8-11*).

In these verses the psalmist has encompassed some six hundred years of the panorama of history that had one single purpose: to sustain God's covenant relationship with his chosen people. God over these centuries was showing how he felt towards the men he had created. He is all the time revealing himself in history. From the wanderings beginning at Ur to the Joseph saga and the sojourn in Egypt, and then in more detail the miraculous deliverance of the Exodus followed by his leading through the desert wilderness, so the psalm unfolds the nation's history. All this

> For he remembered his holy promise,
>     and Abraham his servant (Ps. 105.*42*).

This revelation of his will through the events of history continues throughout the nation's chequered career, including the experience of Exile and the Return. So we read of the exiles

facing the new situation of being estranged from their homeland
and their sacred temple:

> How shall we sing the Lord's song
>   in a foreign land?
> If I forget you, O Jerusalem,
>   let my right hand wither!
> Let my tongue cleave to the roof of my mouth,
>   if I do not remember you,
> if I do not set Jerusalem
>   above my highest joy! (Ps. 137.4-6).

Yet this too was a revelation of God. They came to realise
that God was in the experience of Exile and through it he revealed
that he was not a local tribal god but the only God for every man
and every nation. The Hebrews through this experience found
that God was greater than they had thought and so they learned
through this tragic episode of their history one of the greatest
insights of God's revelation. This is the realisation of what Israel's
future role should be—to become God's Suffering Servant to the
whole world.

> As many were astonished at him—
>   his appearance was so marred, beyond human semblance,
> and his form beyond that of the sons of men—
>   so shall he startle many nations;
> kings shall shut their mouths because of him;
>   for that which has not been told them they shall see,
> and that which they have not heard they shall understand (Is. 52.14-15).

This will be the reaction of the nations of the world to God's
self-revelation of his purpose through the apparently insignificant
history of a small puny people whose leaders had been deported.
God used the Exile to reveal the way ahead for his people—they
were to be his instrument to save the world, through their
tragic history rather than in spite of it.

## GOD REVEALS HIMSELF THROUGH LAW

A third means used by God to reveal himself is that of the *Torah*—the great word that is a symbol to the Hebrew of all his longings and hopes. The word Torah is usually translated 'Law', but we must hasten to add that it means much more than a set of legal enactments, some external regulations. Its richness of meaning can be seen in Psalm 19 which was originally made up of two hymns in praise of Creation and Law respectively. They are linked because Creation and Law are both spheres of God's revelation. Specially significant are the following verses:

> The law of the Lord is perfect, reviving the soul;
> the testimony of the Lord is sure, making wise the simple;
> the precepts of the Lord are right, rejoicing the heart;
> the commandment of the Lord is pure, enlightening the eyes;
> the fear of the Lord is clean, enduring for ever;
> the ordinances of the Lord are true, and righteous altogether.
> More to be desired are they than gold, even much fine gold;
> sweeter also than honey
> and drippings of the honeycomb (Ps. 19.7-10).

We may notice the accumulation of terms used to describe the Law of God and the wealth of his descriptive imagery. The psalmist heaps terms up to convey some part of what the Law means to him—law, testimony, precepts, commandments, word and ordinances. To this we add the characterisation of the Law as perfect, sure, right, pure, clean, true and righteous altogether! Such a Law must be dominant in the psalmist's life when we consider further its power, as he sees it, to refresh the spirit, give wisdom, bring joy to the heart, illumine the mind and create a sense of abiding certainty in life! Such a view of God's Law is a witness to what the psalmist thought of God behind the Law. Every phrase is evidence of a relationship between God and man rather than any contracted, legal agreement that could, in given circumstances, become null and void. No wonder that we have the verdict that the Law is a treasure even beyond the finest gold.


### Law as a Way of Life

One of the most characteristic features of the use of the word Law (*Torah*) is that it is linked with the word for 'Way'. The original for Law comes from a word that means to point at or out. This sense of direction becomes what we now call a directive. So Moses speaks:

> When they have a dispute, they come to me and I decide between a man and his neighbour and I make them know the statutes of God and his decisions (Ex. 18.*16*).

The original for 'decisions' is *toroth* (plural of *torah*)—they are God's directives and they become the law of God. The idea of direction becomes crystallised in the actual way or path in which a man must walk because God has revealed his Way.

> Blessed is the man
>   who walks not in the counsel of the wicked,
> nor stands in the way of sinners,
>   nor sits in the seat of scoffers;
> but his delight is in the law (*torah*) of the Lord,
>   and on his law (*torah*) he meditates day and night . . .
> for the Lord knows the way of the righteous
>   but the way of the wicked will perish (Ps. 1.*1-2,6*).

The Law (*Torah*) has become a way of life that bears witness to the will of God as revealed in his decisions. From being a record of what God wants from his people, the Law has acquired another dimension. It is now a revelation of God to those with whom he has an abiding relationship. It has been pertinently said 'that fundamentally *torah* in the Old Testament denotes God's *revelational decision* and points to the guidance that God would give His people in their everyday life. . . . A translation of *torah* by "word of revelation" would come closer to the original meaning' (T. C. Vriezen, *An Outline of Old Testament Theology*, p. 256; see also for a fuller treatment of the *Torah*, H. Mowvley, *The Testimony of Israel*, ch. 3).

## GOD REVEALS HIMSELF THROUGH
## EXTENSIONS OF HIS PERSONALITY

One of the greatest of the acknowledged insights gained into the Hebrew way of thought through recent research, is that it is able to grasp the idea of wholeness or totality. Sometimes this is called 'corporate personality'. Thus the Israelites saw a man's name, his uttered word, or his property, his clothing, or his native city as all part of one personality. A man has a number of extensions of his personality such as his uttered word that cannot be separated from the man himself. A man is what he says. As with man so with God.

### Through His Word

God's Word is an extension of God and in many passages stands for God in Person. This feature of an extended personality is well illustrated in the following passage.

> For the rain and the snow
>   come down from heaven,
> and return not thither but water the earth,
>   making it bring forth and sprout,
> giving seed to the sower and bread to the eater,
>   so shall my word be that goes forth from my mouth;
> it shall not return to me empty,
>   but it shall accomplish that which I purpose,
> and prosper in the thing for which I sent it (Is. 55.*10-11*).

Repeatedly in the account of God's commissioning of his spokesmen we read of the coming of the Word of the Lord as, for example, he came to Jeremiah.

> Before I formed you in the womb I knew you,
> and before you were born, I consecrated you;
> I appointed you a prophet to the nations (Jer. 1.*5*).

Similar words are used of God's call to Jonah, Micah and Hosea (Jonah 1.*1*; Micah 1.*1*; Hosea 1.*1*). This is the Hebrew way of saying that God himself came to these men in direct personal encounter. These man had no doubt that through his word, what he laid upon their hearts to say to their generation, God was personally revealing his will and purpose.

*Through His Name*

Another extension of God's Personality is his 'Name'. This is a special instance of the power thought to reside in the spoken word. The word uttered by a man may be of positive benefit, as in a blessing, but also harmful or negative, as in a curse. So the word comes to be seen as an extension of the man. So, too, with God. The 'name' is a special example of a word that has power. To know a man's name is to have a relationship with a man and to have some power and control over him. We see this in Jacob's wrestling with the angel of God at Peniel (Gen. 32.*24-30*) and in Moses' request that God should disclose his name at the encounter before the Burning Bush (Exod. 3.*13-14*). The greatest tragedy that could happen to man is that his name should cease to exist. Similarly, the 'Name' of God is an extension of God's Personality, and through 'knowing' his name the Israelites came to a deeper knowledge of his revealed purpose.

Three examples of this emphasis upon God's Name are found in Genesis, the Code of Deuteronomy and in the Psalter.

In Genesis we have the first reference to 'calling on the name' of God, which is clearly a technical term for religious observances (Gen. 4.*26*; 12.*8*), and in Deuteronomy we have a repeated description of the sanctuary in words such as:

> But you shall seek the place which the Lord your God will choose out of all your tribes to put his name and make his habitation there (Deut. 12.*5*; see also vv. *11, 21*).

Where his Name is, God is, and there he meets with his people. The psalmist, too, calls upon the 'Name' of God:

> The Lord answer you in the day of trouble!
>   The name of the God of Jacob protect you!
> May he send you help from the sanctuary,
>   and give you support from Zion!
>
> .       .       .       .       .       .       .       .
>
> Some boast of chariots, and some of horses;
>   but we boast of the name of the Lord our God.
> They will collapse and fall;
>   but we shall rise and stand upright (Ps. 20.*1-2,7-8*; see also Ps. 54).

Another aspect of the Israelites 'calling upon the Name' of God is that it implies that God proclaiming his name to his people is equivalent to his 'claiming and electing the people of Israel to be the "people of Yahweh" '. (See esp. A. Weiser, *The Psalms*, pp. 30–31, 41–42.)

*Through His Glory*

The Personality of God is revealed also through another 'extension' called his 'Glory'. Of particular importance in looking at the reality of the Hebrew phrase 'the glory of God' is to note the link that exists between God himself in person and his glory. A number of passages are only intelligible if we realise that they can be different ways of saying God—that God and his glory are identical.

Isaiah, during the experience of receiving his call from God in the Temple, describes the scene of the seraphim crying one to another:

> Holy, holy, holy, is the Lord of hosts; the whole earth is full of his glory (Is. 6.3).

In commenting on this passage the author of John's Gospel writes: 'Isaiah said this because he saw his glory and spoke of him' (Jn. 12.41). Clearly this use of Glory must mean that God reveals himself in a way that a man can experience. The Glory of God stands for the presence of God. Similarly when Phinehas names her child I-chabod there is a deliberate symbolism behind such a name. The word is made up of the Hebrew word for glory (*Kabod*) and a negative prefixed to it. That is, no glory! All because the Ark of God has been captured and the absence of the Ark is equated to the absence of God. No God, then no glory. (See Ezekiel 9.3-4 for another example of glory signifying the Presence of God, and Exod. 24.16, 2 Chron. 5.14 for glory as a means of God guiding his people.)

*Through His Face*

We shall see below as we consider some of the insights of Hebrew psychology that there is a frequent emphasis laid upon the parts of the human body, such as the eyes, hand, arm or the heart and the internal organs. Although physical organs they are referred to by the Old Testament writers in a way that expresses the various feelings and mental states of the person, whether man or God. The face especially is clearly an index of personality in its various moods. In Ps. 104.15 a man's face indicates his gladness, whilst in Gen. 4.5, the reference to the face of Cain signifies anger.

In a number of passages the face of God is mentioned in such a way that we readily see that the writer means us to understand by the phrase an extension of the personality of God—His Face!

At the desert rendezvous of God, the Tent of Meeting, Moses using the right of a friend to speak face to face, demands that God outlines his future plans for his people in the wilderness situation. In reply God gives answer:

> And he said, 'My presence will go with you and I will give you rest'
> And he said to him, 'If thy presence (*panim*-face) will not go with me, do not carry us up from here' (Ex. 33.14-15).

The 'face of God' is used to signify the presence of God himself in the midst of his people. Similarly, when the Deuteronomic writer comes to interpret the great deliverance at the Exodus from Egypt he writes:

> And because he loved your fathers and chose their descendants after them, and brought you out of Egypt with his own presence (*panim*-face) by his great power . . . (Deut. 4.37).

This phrase 'with his own presence' in the original is literally 'with his face'. The writer is anxious to get his point over—they had been delivered by God in person, not an intermediary.

### The face of God as a revelation of himself

There is a further emphasis in the Hebrew phrase 'face of God'. It is used to express both the purpose of the cultic rites of the Temple and also the personal devotions of the individual. The psalmist cries out:

> O God, thou art my God, I seek thee,
>     my soul thirsts for thee;
> my flesh faints for thee,
>     as in a dry and weary land where no water is.

> So I have looked upon thee in the sanctuary,
>   beholding thy power and glory (Ps. 63. *1-2*).

The phrase 'looked upon thee' presupposes the idea of the face of God and in another psalm the actual word is used:

> As for me, I shall behold thy face in righteousness,
>   when I awake I shall be satisfied with beholding thy form (Ps. 17.*15*;
>   see also Ps. 42.*2*; 27.*7-9*).

So the 'Face of God' is a means by which God reveals himself.

### FOR FURTHER READING

W. EICHRODT, *Theology of the Old Testament* (II, S.C.M., 1967).

G. VON RAD, *Genesis* (S.C.M., 1961).

A. R. JOHNSON, *The One and the Many in the Israelite Conception of God* (Univ. of Wales Press, 1942).

A. WEISER, *The Psalms* (S.C.M., 1962).

PART THREE

# THE RESPONSE OF MAN

# 6

# ORIGIN AND CREATION OF MAN

HAVING seen, in part at least, the broad outlines of the way in which the Old Testament affirms that God reveals himself to man we turn to ask, how does man respond to this initiative of God? The answer will clearly depend on what man is; his nature will decide his actions and reaction.

## CREATED IN THE IMAGE OF GOD

Made in the image of God. This astounding claim is made on man's behalf in only three passages, the first reading:

> Then God said, 'Let us make man in our image, after our likeness; and let them have dominion over the fish of the sea. . . .'
> So God created man in his own image, in the image of God he created him (Gen. 1.26-27; see also Gen. 5.1-3; 9.6).

A striking feature of these passages is that they all occur in the source behind the book of Genesis, that has been called the 'Priestly' one. The emphasis in this document is upon the transcendence of God, the distance between God and man, yet here, thrice repeated, man and God are seen in an intimate, near relationship. In what does the image or likeness consist? Various answers have been given—man's upright stature, his intelligence or ability to speak, his freedom or spiritual capacity. The key is found in the two terms used, 'image' and 'likeness'. The second word gives a precision to the first. The image is to resemble or be like the original. In this context, this can only mean man is to be like God (not by any means to be understood as equal to God). The phrase 'in the image of God' is best understood against the background of the Ancient Near East. It was frequent for a king to set up an image in remote provinces of an empire where he would never appear in person. The statue would represent the King and, in the thought of the East, would be the King. So we frequently meet the Assyrian inscription: 'I will set up my statue in their midst'. The image is the equivalent of an ambassador. This then, is the plain meaning of the text; man, that is, every man, not a special kind of man like a king, but the ordinary variety, is the ambassador of God on earth, to represent God to the rest of the universe. (See especially Von Rad, *Genesis*, pp. 55–59.)

The whole function of the representative is to be able to communicate the mind and will of the one he represents. The purpose of God making man in his own image is that he should by his response, communicate the will and purpose of God. This is the noblest gift that God could give, a gift that is fully seen in the Incarnation of Christ, but which, in part, God has already given to every man.

As God's revelation continued, he showed more of his will and purpose through psalmist and prophet. As men responded, the image of God became progressively realised. Man was sharing in communion with God.

## DOMINION OVER CREATION

One of the best expressions of what is meant by being made in the image of God is found in Psalm 8:

What is man that thou art mindful of him,
  and the son of man that thou dost care for him?
Yet thou hast made him little less than God
  and dost crown him with glory and honour.
Thou hast given him dominion over the works of thy hands;
  thou hast put all things under his feet (Ps. 8.4-6).

It is not accidental that both in Gen. 1.27 and also Ps. 8.6, the writer passes immediately from affirming that God has given this gift to man, of being made in his image, to a commissioning.

And let them have dominion over the fish of the sea, and over the birds of the air, and over the cattle, and over all the earth, and over every creeping thing that creeps upon the earth (Gen. 1.26; see also Ps. 8.6-8).

Yet the commission to rule, to have dominion, is not the essence of being made in the image of God. There is no suggestion of mankind being invited to become *Herrenvolk* (master race) in relation to God's world. Rather, the way that man exercises his power to rule either expresses or diminishes the image of God. As the relationship between God and man deepens the 'image of God' is seen more clearly. Man is commissioned for power but it is derived power and must be rededicated to the Giver and his creation. It is, in the end, power on behalf of, not power over.

So far we have looked only at the passage in the creation story but the other two references to the 'image of God' are significant not only for their use of the same phrase but because of the specific contexts. They read:

This is the book of the generations of Adam. When God created man, he made him in the likeness of God (Gen. 5.1).

But this account could only have been written after the account of Genesis ch.3 with its description of man's alienation from God and expulsion from Eden. Yet the writer feels that he must retain the reference to man and the likeness of God. Similarly, in Gen. 9.6 we read:

> Whoever sheds the blood of man, by man shall his blood be shed, for God made man in his own image.

The whole point of these two instances of the phrase 'in the likeness or image of God' is that they occur after the spiritual experiences represented by the Fall and the Flood and still it is not said that the image of God has been destroyed. This means that the 'image of God' in man was never intended to suggest a state of perfect rightness in man himself. Rather, that God has created man to be in a relationship with himself.

This is the real vocation of man—to be the image of God. Sin is real but its occurrence does not cancel automatically the relationship between God and man. The image of God in man continues because it rests on God's purpose. Sin impairs but never removes or obliterates the image of God. The face of the coin is defaced but never completely destroyed.

### MAN IN REVOLT AND ALIENATION

We have seen that God takes the initiative in revealing himself to man. Further, that without making the mistake of making man equal to God, we realise that there is a kinship, a communion of will and purpose with God, that is open to man. Yet how does man react to God's gracious action? The early stories of Genesis give us the key. He cannot stand in the presence of God, he must hide himself. The examples of Adam and Cain both underline this feature of man's alienation:

> But the Lord God called to the man, and said to him, 'Where are you?' And he said, 'I heard the sound of thee in the garden, and I was afraid because I was naked, and I hid myself' (Gen. 3.9-10).

Through the genius of the Hebrew mind we see the recurring human situation that is mirrored in this chapter, the inability of man to accept his creaturehood, the urge to be like God. This is a perversion of what we meant by being made in the image of God. It is because of this perennial experience that mankind is driven away from the presence of God as too spiritually dangerous. So we read the closing verses of the Story of the Fall:

> Then the Lord God said:
> 'Behold, the man has become like one of us, knowing good and evil; and now lest he put forth his hand and take also of the tree of life, and eat, and live for ever'—therefore the Lord God sent him forth from the garden of Eden, to till the ground from which he was taken (Gen. 3.22-23).

Here behind the parable of all human experience we are dealing with abiding and contemporary truth. For we can make this insight our own: 'Eden is on no map, and Adam's fall fits no historical calendar. Moses is not nearer to the Fall than we are, because he lived three thousand years before our time. The Fall refers not to some datable aboriginal calamity in the historic past of humanity, but to a dimension of human experience which is always present—namely that we who have been created for fellowship with God repudiate it continually; and that the whole of mankind does this along with us' (J. S. Whale, *Christian Doctrine*, p. 52; Fontana edition p. 49).

The result of this repudiation of fellowship with God is that man finds himself an outsider—he has become alienated because of his revolt.

The same theme is stressed as we read of the sequel to Cain's murder of his brother Abel as God gives his judgement:

> When you till the ground it shall no longer yield to you its strength; ye shall be a fugitive and a wanderer on the earth. Cain said to the Lord, 'My punishment is greater than I can bear. Behold, thou hast driven me this day away from the ground; and from thy face I shall be hidden; and I shall be a fugitive and a wanderer on the earth' (Gen. 4.12-14).

This is the way that the creation of man worked out. He became a fugitive from the face, that is the Presence, of God! The essence of sin is just this—that we alienate ourselves from the only relationship that expresses our true nature, by claiming for ourselves what belongs only to God.


## THE VOCABULARY OF SIN

The Old Testament, in seeking to describe this basic fact about man, that he puts himself against God, uses a number of distinct terms, carrying different overtones.


### Missing the Mark

The most frequently used word for sin is one that is used of missing a set target. In the description of the forces of the tribe of Benjamin we read:

> Among all these were seven hundred picked men who were left-handed; every one could sling a stone at a hair, and not miss. (Judg. 20.*16*).

The word translated 'miss' is later used of man committing sin against God and his fellows. Also in Proverbs the same word is used:

> It is not good for man to be without knowledge,
> and he who makes haste with his feet misses his way (Prov. 19.*2*).

Another illustration of the basic idea of missing or falling short of a target is found in the comfort that Eliphaz, the Elder Statesman among the Friends, seeks to give Job when he promises:

> You shall know that your tent is safe,
> and you shall inspect your fold and miss nothing (Job 5.*24*).

The phrase 'miss nothing' employs the same verb that is used to describe man's sinning. Here it is a question of being short of a given number. The standard is not reached. Sin thus has an element of failing to reach a moral standard.

## Sin as a twisting or perverting

The second term used for man's sinning has an original sense of twisting or bending. This is expressed by our word perversion. In the prophet Jeremiah we read of his pleading that Israel might return to God:

A voice on the bare heights is heard,
   the weeping and pleading of Israel's sons,
because they have perverted their way,
   they have forgotten the Lord their God (Jer. 3.21).

The relationship between God and his people has been distorted, twisted from God's original purpose for them.

Similarly, when Elihu describes the consequences if Job would but accept his suffering as a chastening from God he says:

Then man prays to God, and he accepts him,
   he comes into his presence with joy.
He recounts to men his salvation,
   and he sings before men, and says:
'I sinned, and perverted what was right,
   and it was not requited to me' (Job 33.26-27).

Here sin is seen as a twisting and perverting of God-given powers.

## Sin as an act of personal rebellion

A third term used for sin, and the most profound, carries a meaning of personal rebellion. It is used of one person who rebels against another. So we find it used of a son's revolt against his father (Is. 1.2) and of rebellion against the law of God:

Set the trumpet to your lips,
   for a vulture is over the house of the Lord,
because they have broken my covenant,
   and transgressed my law (Hos. 8.1).

The covenant relationship initiated by God is violated by Israel. In one of the penitential psalms we see the essence of the estrangement and rebellion.

> For I know my transgressions,
>     and my sin is ever before me.
> Against thee, thee only, have I sinned,
>     and done that which is evil in thy sight (Ps. 51.*3-4*).

Sin, at its most personal level, is always 'against thee, thee only'. (See also Luke 15.*18*.)

Missing the mark, perverting or twisting what is originally straight, violating a relationship. These are the main emphases in the Hebrew vocabulary of sin.

## FOR FURTHER READING

W. EICHRODT, *Theology of the Old Testament*, II, (S.C.M., 1967).

E. JACOB, *Theology of the Old Testament* (Hodder & Stoughton, 1958).

G. VON RAD, *Genesis* (S.C.M., 1961).

C. RYDEN SMITH, *The Bible Doctrine of Sin and of the Ways of God* (Epworth, 1953).

# 7

## THE NATURE OF MAN

In thinking of the way in which God reveals himself we have already encountered the idea of personality going beyond the physical frame to include extensions such as name, face, possessions, clothes, that are all part of the whole that we may call the self.

Specially significant are the terms, flesh, living soul and spirit, which are used continually to describe man and we shall now look at the main emphasis and import of each one.

### MAN IS FLESH

The term for flesh (*basar*) is used of what man has in common with other living beings. It is the stuff or raw material of life and without it the Hebrew mind could not think of man existing. This is the reason why, centuries later, Paul wrestles with the dilemma of trying to express what the Resurrection meant to him and is forced to speak of a spiritual body:

> It is sown a physical body, it is raised a spiritual body. If there is a physical body, there is also a spiritual body (1 Cor. 15.44).

It is impossible for Paul, a Hebrew of the Hebrews, to visualise any disembodied spirit so he must think of a body even if he must call it spiritual!

Having said that man is flesh, we must hasten to add that he is also much more. Before he becomes a living creature the breath of life must be present.

> Then the Lord God formed man of dust from the ground, and breathed into his nostrils the breath of life; and man became a living being (Gen. 2.7; see also Gen. 6.17; 7.15; 9.15).

The term can also be used to express the spiritual faculties and attitudes. The great error to be avoided is to equate 'flesh' as it occurs in the Old Testament with the materialism or radical division of later thought of man into either two or three distinct parts, such as flesh and spirit or even body, soul and mind. Such an approach is quite alien to the Hebrew characteristic of seeing things as a whole. So we read in the psalms:

> My soul longs, yea, faints
>    for the courts of the Lord;
> my heart and flesh sing for joy
>    to the living God. (Ps. 84.2).

> Therefore my heart is glad, and my soul rejoices;
>    my body also dwells secure (Ps. 16.9).

The interchangeability of the terms 'flesh', 'soul' and 'body' illustrates the way that wholeness or corporate personality is such a natural manner of thinking to the Old Testament writers. Today we would say that the psalmist is speaking about his self. Two further associations are worth noting:

*Flesh as symbol of Weakness*

An outstanding example of this characteristic use of 'flesh' as signifying weakness is found in the warning of Isaiah against reliance upon military pacts and negotiations to save the nation instead of trust in God.

Woe to those who go down to Egypt for help
   and rely on horses,
who trust in chariots because they are many
   and in horsemen because they are very strong,
but do not look to the Holy One of Israel
   or consult the Lord!

.     .     .     .     .     .     .

The Egyptians are men, and not God;
   and their horses are flesh, and not spirit (Is. 31.*1,3*).

The parallelism (that is, of thought, not of sound as in Western poetry) clearly shows that flesh is linked with man and spirit with God and the main burden of the passage is to underline the poverty of man's weakness when opposed by the majesty of God's strength.


*Flesh and Impulse to Sin*

In later thought, especially under Greek influence, there is a frequent connection made between flesh and sin as if the source of sin was in being made of flesh. Yet there is no foundation for this in the Old Testament and the idea is not found until the apocryphal books are written. In the *Wisdom of Solomon* we read:

Because wisdom will not enter a deceitful soul,
   nor dwell in a body enslaved to sin (Wisdom of Solomon 1.*4*).

But this is to reflect a later way of thinking in which matter or flesh is evil in itself and so the source of sin. Yet the Old Testament verdict of God upon his created world which included matter and flesh is that it was very good (Gen. 1.*31*). In Gen. 3 the Story of the Fall hinges upon man's spiritual arrogance in wanting to be equal to God not upon his being flesh.

## MAN IS A LIVING SOUL

One of the most significant terms used in describing the Hebrew idea of man is usually translated 'soul' or living being. This word *nephesh* is found in the creation narrative:

> Then the Lord God formed man of dust from the ground, and breathed into his nostrils the breath of life; and man became a living being (*nephesh*) (Gen. 2.7).

The word is the Old Testament counterpart of the Greek *psyche* (soul) which is familiar in the words of ordinary usage today, such as psychology—the word about the soul or mind. This parallel with the Greek term must serve as a warning. There is no two-fold division of man into body and soul in the Old Testament, but man is a unity of body, soul and spirit, as our next section will show. To the Hebrew mind it is a question of 'Both—And' not 'Either—Or'.

### *The Soul as Breath of Life*

The original meaning of soul (*nephesh*) is found in such passages as

> Therefore Sheol has enlarged its throat [R.S.V. appetite]
>   and opened its mouth beyond measure,
> and the nobility of Jerusalem and her multitude go down,
>   her throng and he who exults in her (Is. 5.*14*).

Here we have the clear meaning of 'throat' while the associated meaning of 'neck' is found in the psalm from the Book of Jonah:

> The waters encompassed me up to the neck, ('closed in over me', R.S.V.)
>   the deep was round about me;
> weeds were wrapped about my head (Jonah 2.*5*).

The transition from throat to breath and so to being alive may be readily seen in the expression 'to breathe out the soul' (*nephesh*) as a term for dying.

> But the eyes of the wicked will fail;
>   all way of escape will be lost to them,
> and their hope is to breathe their last (Job 11.*20*).

## The Soul and the Will

In a number of passages we find the term we are examining clearly used to express the dominant will and purpose of a person. In the time of Hosea the neglect and distortion of their calling by the so-called priests leads to the prophet's bitter comment:

> They feed on the sin of my people;
>   they are greedy for their iniquity (Hos. 4.*8*).

The actual original for 'they are greedy for' is 'they lift up their *nephesh* (throat)' and this graphically portrays the panting desire for evil by a decadent priesthood. So, too, in the account of the anointing of Jehu as King of Israel. The trumpets have sounded and he has been acclaimed, then he is commissioned to destroy Jezebel. The text reads:

> If this is your mind, then let no one slip out of the city to go and tell the news in Jezreel (2 Kings 9.*15*).

'If this is your mind' is literally 'if this is your soul' (*nephesh*) certainly meaning 'if this is what you want, your purpose', that I should be King.

## The Soul and the Self

A further use of our key word is to express what we today would call the personality or the self. A recent comment has been 'In numerous passages—135 have been counted—the most adequate translation of *nephesh* (soul) is the personal pronoun with which moreover it is sometimes used in parallel:

> We have escaped as a bird from the snare of the fowlers; the snare is broken and we have escaped (Ps. 124.7)'.

(E. Jacob, *Theology of the Old Testament*, p.161).

The pronoun 'we' is literally 'our soul' and indicates two features. First, that once again we see the corporate nature of Hebrew thought because 'soul' or 'self' is in the singular and secondly, the parallelism between 'soul' and 'we' supports the identifying in many instances of 'soul' with the personal pronoun. (See also Num. 23.*10*; Job 30.*25*.) The same equation is found in legal contexts when cases are cited of the penalty to be exacted if any one offends against a particular law:

> Whoever eats any blood, that person shall be cut off from his people (Lev. 7.27; see also vv. *21,20*).

The 'person' translates 'soul' or better 'self'. The 'soul' can therefore mean what we mean by self.

## MAN AND HIS SPIRIT

To complete the sketch of the nature of man we turn to consider the significance of spirit (*ruach*). The original meaning of the word translated 'spirit' is 'air in motion' and so it can be used of both 'wind' and 'spirit'. The same double role is played by the New Testament word for 'spirit', *pneuma*, which is easily recognisable as an element in such contexts as 'pneumatic' drill or tyre, with the meaning 'wind'. Here the main characteristics of the Old Testament usage can be commented on.

### God is the only source of man's spirit

The Bible knows nothing of spirit with a small *s* that man

can produce for himself through some specialised technique. The Spirit is the gift of God and is only fully possessed by God.

We read of God's gift of the spirit to men in such passages as the coming of the Spirit of God upon Samson:

> And the Spirit of the Lord came mightily upon him, and he tore the lion asunder as one tears a kid; and he had nothing in his hand (Judg. 14.6).

Similarly, the clash between Israelites and the Amalekites and the Midianites in the Valley of Jezreel affords another instance of God's gift of his spirit to Gideon:

> But the Spirit of the Lord took possession of Gideon; and he sounded the trumpet (Judg. 6.34).

These passages underline the second fact that emerges from the use of spirit and his coming from God, that is, the element of dynamic power connected with its onset.

*Man's Spirit and Spiritual Endowment*

Although, in some of the earlier passages, the emphasis is upon the abnormal, extraordinary feats that God's gift enables a man to do, there is the other side of the coin. The God-given spirit can express itself in the skilled craftsmanship of the man who lovingly devotes his skill to the furnishing of the Ark and the Tent of Meeting and the Mercy seat with all the sacred utensils.

> And I have filled him with the Spirit of God, and with ability and intelligence, with knowledge and all craftsmanship, to devise artistic designs to work in gold, silver and bronze, in cutting stones for setting, and in carving wood, for work in every craft (Ex. 31.3-5).

So, too, the psalmist speaks of man's spirit that expresses itself in qualities of heart and mind that owe everything to God's gift of the spirit.

Create in me a clean heart, O God,
  and put a new and right spirit within me,
Cast me not away from thy presence,
  and take not thy holy Spirit from me.
Restore to me the joy of thy salvation,
  and uphold me with a willing spirit (Ps. 51.*10-12*).

The same characteristic use of spirit is found in the description
of the spiritual endowment of the servant portrayed in Isaiah:

And the Spirit of the Lord shall rest upon him,
  the spirit of wisdom and understanding,
the spirit of counsel and might,
  the spirit of knowledge and the fear of the Lord (Is. 11.*2*; see also Is.
  42.*1*; Zech 4.*6*).

A significant comment on the working of the spirit in man has
been made by Pedersen, 'the spirit is more particularly the motive
power of the soul . . .'. The heart and the spirit act upon the centre
and urge it in a certain direction, towards action.

Every one whose heart stirred him up, and everyone whom his spirit
made willing came and brought Yahweh's offering (Ex. 35.*21*).
(See J. Pedersen, *Israel, Its Life and Culture*, I–II, p.104.

### INSIGHTS OF HEBREW PSYCHOLOGY

From this brief sketch of the nature of man with its special
emphasis on flesh, soul and spirit, we may bring together in
summary a number of insights into the character of Hebrew
psychology.

*First, that there is no opposition or separation between body
and soul or even a further elaboration of a three-fold division
into body, soul and spirit*

Man is not a being with separate parts but is always thought of as a whole, a totality. This grasp of the whole is expressed admirably in the daily prayer called the *Shema* (this is actually the first word of the verse in Hebrew)

> Hear, O Israel: The Lord our God is one Lord; and you shall love the Lord your God with all your heart, and with all your soul, and with all your might (Deut. 6.4).

*Secondly, man in Israelite thought is one unit of living power*

The different physical parts of the body such as bones, heart, bowels and kidneys, the flesh and the blood are all spoken of as possessing psychical properties. So the psalmist gripped with fear expresses this emotion in these words:

> I am poured out like water,
>    and all my bones are out of joint;
> my heart is like wax,
>    it is melted within my breast (Ps. 22.14).

Here the physical is used to express the psychology of man's emotions, attitudes and feelings.

*Thirdly, the heart is used to express a man's mind and purpose*

This, of course, is in contrast to the predominant emphasis on the affection and emotions that the word 'heart' has for the Western mind.

So the prophet Hosea speaks of the fatal fascination that reliance upon political treaties with Egypt or Assyria has for many of the nation's leaders:

> Ephraim is like a dove,
>    silly and without sense,
> calling to Egypt, going to Assyria (Hos. 7.11).

The original for 'without sense' literally means 'without heart'.

So often we can be saved from an emotional interpretation of a given passage by the realisation that heart carries an emphasis upon will and intellect more than emotion and affection.

*Finally, the physical part of a man is often used to express the whole personality*

The references to the face, the eyes, the arm, the bones or the head, although apparently only to a part of the physical frame are often to be understood as meaning the whole person. This applies both to men and God.

> Fill me with joy and gladness;
>    let the bones which thou hast broken rejoice.
> Hide thy face from my sins,
>    and blot out all my iniquities (Ps. 51.*8-9*).

> Where is he who put in the midst of them
>    his holy Spirit
> who caused his glorious arm
>    to go at the right hand of Moses (Is. 63.*11-12*).

In these passages 'bones' and 'arm' stand for the personality of the psalmist and God respectively.

FOR FURTHER READING

A. R. JOHNSON, *The Vitality of the Individual in the Thought of Ancient Israel* (Univ. of Wales Press, 1949).

G. A. F. KNIGHT, *A Christian Theology of the Old Testament* (S.C.M., 1959).

H. W. ROBINSON, art. *Hebrew Psychology* in *The People and the Book* (ed. A. S. Peake, Oxford, 1925).

H. W. ROBINSON, *Inspiration and Revelation* (Oxford, 1946).

# 8

## MAN AND THE CULT

BECAUSE of Man's revolt against God's will and purpose and his alienation from God the need arises of a means whereby the two can be reconciled, the relationship restored. On God's side the desire and purpose is clear—he seeks to redeem and save. For man he seeks to find ways and means of reaching God and re-establishing the broken fellowship. So Koehler comments, 'The cult was originally man's attempt to express to God his gratitude, his supplications, his confession, his desire to atone, his excuses, his worship' (*Old Testament Theology*, p. 197).

The heart of the cult organisation concerns the variety of different ways in which the universal practice of sacrifice may be performed. The questions arise immediately what is sacrifice, how did it start, what is its essential nature? To these questions we turn.

### THE ORIGIN OF SACRIFICE AND ITS NATURE

As we seek to discover the thinking behind the sacrificial act we must readily realise that we shall not find one original type and the temptation to be resisted, is that of forcing the evidence into one particular mould. The existence of this attempt on man's part to maintain a relationship with divine beings is part of the story of man in every age and place. 'The hunter, who places part of his kill in the forest in grateful recognition of the divine power that sent the game his way; the farmer who consecrates the first produce of his fields to the god who, according to his belief, made the crops grow; the Babylonian sufferer who gives a lamb to the gods to ransom himself from the sin he supposes to be the cause of his suffering; the Mexican Aztec who kills a young man and offers his heart to the sun-god in order to secure the vital forces of the sun for the land; the Moabite King Mesha who offers his son to his national god in order to win a victory over the attacking Israelites (2 Kings 3.27); all these, and thousands of others, are examples of the world-wide religious practice we refer to as sacrifice' (H. Ringgren, *Sacrifice in the Bible*, p. 7).

### SACRIFICE AS GIFT AND TRIBUTE

One dominant motive behind the offering of a sacrifice to God may be seen in the bringing of a gift or tribute. We see this in the directives given by the Deuteronomic Code to govern the conduct of God's people after entry to Canaan.

> When you come into the land which the Lord your God gives you for an inheritance, and have taken possession of it, and live in it, you shall take some of the first of all the fruit of the ground, which you harvest from your land that the Lord your God gives you, and you shall put it in a basket, and you shall go to the place which the Lord your God will choose, to make his name dwell there (Deut. 26. *1-2* see also *10-11*, Ex. 13.*2,13*; 22.*29*).

It is probable that an early part of this bringing of gifts to the deity was the need to give food to the gods; and by making provision for the gods, they in turn would respond by granting their favours to man.

The very vehemence of the Psalmist's rejection of this idea of

God underlines the prevalence of so thinking of God as if he could be made more amenable to man by such offers of food.

> I do not reprove you for your sacrifices;
>     your burnt offerings are continually before me.
> I will accept no bull from your house,
>     nor he-goat from your folds.
> For every beast of the forest is mine,
>     the cattle on a thousand hills.
> I know all the birds of the air,
>     and all that moves in the field is mine.
> If I were hungry, I would not tell you;
>     for the world and all that is in it is mine.
> Do I eat the flesh of bulls,
>     or drink the blood of goats? (Ps. 50.*8-13*).

Here the psalmist is attacking the spiritual arrogance and presumption that almost assumes that man could exert pressure upon God.

This idea of providing sustenance comes in time to be refined and the bringing of gifts can quite genuinely be an act of gratitude and a recognition that God is the source of all the gifts that man receives from his world.

At its best, sacrifice is to be seen not as a demand of God upon man that he renders this service but an action that expresses gratitude for what God has done for man.

The psalmists repeatedly sound this note of thanksgiving as a part of their attitude. Their feelings of gratitude impel them to offer sacrifice. That their laws require such sacrifice does not alter the fact that this they themselves want to do.

So the opening lines of Psalm 107 give the key to all that follows:

> O give thanks to the Lord, for he is good;
>     for his steadfast love endures for ever!
> Let the redeemed of the Lord say so . . . (vv. *1-2*).

The psalmist continues describing situations in which members
of the community have experienced the redeeming power of
God. Captives who have known release, the sick who have
regained health, sailors who have known rescue from storm at
sea are all enjoined to turn in gratitude to God:

> Let them thank the Lord for his steadfast love,
>     for his wonderful works to the sons of men!
> And let them offer sacrifices of thanksgiving,
>     and tell of his deeds in songs of joy! (vv. *21-22*).

Through such sacrifice of thanksgiving the whole community
become involved in the religious experience of the individual
and the group. (See also Ps. 27.*6*; 54.*6f*; 56.*12f*.)


## SACRIFICE AS COMMUNION AND FELLOWSHIP

A second theme that is implicit in a number of Old Testament
passages dealing with the offering of sacrifices is that of the sacrificial meal which is shared by God and his worshippers.

Especially significant are the accounts of the peace offering. In
Leviticus ch. 3 we can trace an outline of the procedure originally
laid down for the ritual actions. (See also Leviticus 7.*11-21*.)
The basic meaning of the word translated 'peace' is that of
wholeness, being intact. It seems likely that the purpose behind
this sacrifice is that a relationship between God and his worshippers
might be maintained.

There is presuppposed a communion and fellowship that the
sacrificial meal which is the climax of the peace-offering ritual
helps to establish and maintain. The recurring Bible phrase is
'to eat before the Lord' and we find it in such passages as:

> And there you shall eat before the Lord your God, and you shall rejoice,
> you and your households, in all that you undertake, in which the Lord
> your God has blessed you (Deut. 12.7; see also v.*18*; 14.*23,26*; 15.*20*).

And Jethro, Moses' father-in-law, offered a burnt offering and sacrifices to God; and Aaron came with all the elders of Israel to eat bread with Moses' father-in-law before God (Ex. 18.*12*).

The significance of the phrase 'before the Lord' is only fully grasped when we remember the use of 'face' as an extension of God's personality. The Hebrew preposition 'before' is literally 'at the face of'. That is, God is there and his worshippers are in his presence. A parallel idea is expressed in the theme of communion that underlies the Covenant that is ratified on Sinai through the sacrificial act.

> And he sent young men of the people of Israel, who offered burnt offerings and sacrificed peace offerings of oxen to the Lord. And Moses took half of the blood and put it in basins, and half of the blood he threw against the altar. Then he took the book of the Covenant, and read it in the hearing of the people; and they said, 'All that the Lord has spoken we will do, and we will be obedient.' And Moses took the blood and threw it upon the people, and said, 'Behold the blood of the covenant which the Lord has made with you in accordance with all these words' (Ex. 24.*5-8*).

The account ends with 'they beheld God, and ate and drank' (v.*11*). This seems an unmistakable reference to a sacred meal through which the covenant is confirmed.

The communion and fellowship of God and his people is established through the sacrificial act and the meal. The significance of the blood being thrown on people and altar is that both now share in a common life since the blood is much more a symbol of life than death. (See Lev. 17.*11* and Roger Tomes, *The Fear of the Lord*, ch. 3, for a discussion of covenant and passover.)

### SACRIFICE AND THE REMOVAL OF SINS

A number of sacrifices have the express purpose specifically stated, to remove all that impairs the bond between God and man and to restore the relationship that sin has endangered. These are called sin offerings and guilt offerings. (See especially Lev. chs. 4, 5 and 6.)

The Day of Atonement ritual described in Lev. 16 gives us a vivid picture of the scene on this solemn occasion when the high priest executes the following ritual:

> And when he has made an end of atoning for the holy place and the tent of meeting and the altar, he shall present the live goat; and Aaron shall lay both his hands upon the head of the live goat, and confess over him all the iniquities of the people of Israel and all their transgressions, all their sins; and he shall put them upon the head of the goat, and send him away into the wilderness . . . (vv. *20-21*).

Earlier in the ritual a bull and a goat are killed as a sin offering (vv. *11,15*). The essential purpose is to remove sin through the sacrifice of the sin offering and the transference of a man's sin to the animal—the scapegoat. The precise meaning of the word used for what is now called 'atonement' is 'compensation' for sin.

In all this it is certain that here is no mechanical act that a man can perform without reference to God. It is God who makes this action of man effective.

> For the life of the flesh is in the blood; and I have given it for you upon the altar to make atonement for your souls; for it is the blood that makes atonement by reason of the life (Lev. 17.*11*).

It is highly significant that the sacrifice only becomes effective to the Hebrew mind because of God. It is of his institution. Notice that 'I' (i.e. God) is in the emphatic position of the original. Although through the sacrificial act men are performing a ritual that could be described as 'magical' yet to the Hebrew mind this is not necessarily so. In the ritual of the Day of Atonement that we have glanced at, the precondition of any reality is that the priest should, on behalf of the nation, confess the sins of the people (Lev. 16.*21*).

The spiritual attitude of the one who sacrifices is part of the sacrifice and in the name of God the priest pronounces a word of acceptance that changes the very act of sacrifice from a mechanical way of avoiding the consequences of sin into an instrument of God's grace. Such an acceptance by God is found in the ordinances of the Temple outlined by Ezekiel in his picture of the New Community in which he says:

> Seven days shall they make atonement for the altar and purify it, and so consecrate it. And when they have completed these days, then from the eighth day onward the priests shall offer upon the altar your burnt offerings and your peace offerings; and I will accept you, says the Lord God (Ezek. 43.26-27, see also 20.40f.; 2 Sam. 24.23).

Without this acceptance there is no mechanical effectiveness. The value of any sacrifice must take into account the manner of a man's spiritual approach and, above all, God's response to man's need of communion and fellowship. Sacrifice cannot be the source of communion with God, but only the means.


## COMMUNION OUTSIDE THE CULT

As we complete this brief sketch of the thinking expressed by the act of sacrifice we must go beyond such laws and ritual to consider situations that are recognised as beyond their range of effectiveness.


### Sins with a 'high hand'

A phrase that is often repeated in the Old Testament in the legal sections, refers to those evil actions that are committed 'with a high hand';

> But the person who does anything with a high hand, whether he is native or a sojourner, reviles the Lord, and that person shall be cut off from among his people (Num. 15.30).

By 'with a high hand' the crimes of a deliberate set opposition to God's will are meant, as if the hand is raised in contemptuous defiance of God himself. Yet even this is not the last word, since all the time God has to be reckoned with. As it is God who gives reality to sacrifice, so God must have the final word about the sin of man and the method of man's atoning.

## Intercession and the Removal of Sin

As the impact of the prophetic teaching makes itself felt so we find the strengthening of the personal factor. This applies both to man and God. We see this demonstrated in the number of occasions when God is approached by men who intercede on behalf of their people.

So Abraham intercedes for Sodom (Gen. 18) and Moses for the people who have sinned against God (Exod. 32.30ff.). Similarly, Moses intercedes both for Pharaoh (Exod. 9.17ff.) and for Miriam (Numb. 12.11ff.) and Job for his friends (Job 33.23ff.).

These acts of personal intercession could only come from a relationship between God and man that no cultic ritual could fully express. It is because God is God that atonement is ultimately possible. This note we hear again and again:

> I will not execute my fierce anger,
>     I will not again destroy Ephraim;
> for I am God and not man,
>     the Holy One in your midst
> and I will not come to destroy (Hos. 11.9).

So we understand the pleading behind the prophet's voice:

> Come now, let us reason together, says the Lord:
>     though your sins are like scarlet,
> they shall be as white as snow;
>     though they are red like crimson,
> they shall become like wool (Is. 1.18).

The whole of what the cult seeks to do through sacrifice and the great figures who make personal intercession is ultimately dependent on what God wills and wishes:

> I, I am He,
>> who blots out your trangressions for my own sake,
>> and I will not remember your sins (Is. 43.25).

This is what God wants—and for this reason alone is such restoration of man, the alienated one, possible. God is involved in man's return and initiates the very conditions to bring it about.

### FOR FURTHER READING

A. R. JOHNSON, *The Cultic Prophet in Ancient Israel* (Univ. of Wales Press, 1962).

E. KOEHLER, *Old Testament Theology* (Lutterworth, 1957).

H. RINGGREN, *Sacrifice in the Bible* ( Lutterworth, 1962).

# 9

# MAN IN COMMUNITY

THE Old Testament view of man is in essence a social view. Modern views of man as a private individual are completely without Biblical foundation. It may be agreed that after the prophetic preaching of Jeremiah and Ezekiel there is an emphasis on the personal relationship between man and God. Yet this undoubted truth can be overstated. One must not oppose the individual man and society.

'The fact is that the Bible presents no conception of an individual man as existing in and for himself . . . on the contrary, the individual was created for society—"One man is no man", for he is man only in the midst and as a member of a group. There is no man apart from a people in which he lives and moves and has his being' (G. E. Wright, *The Biblical Doctrine of Man in Society*, p. 47). We shall now examine the evidence for such a verdict and various aspects of man's relationship to the community.

## INDIVIDUAL AND COMMUNITY

The social nature of man is expressed quite clearly in the accounts of his creation in Genesis 1 and 2. The word *'adam* used

in Genesis 1 clearly represents both man and woman, since the
text reads:

> So God created man in his own image, in the image of God he created him;
> male and female he created them (Gen. 1.27).

Here 'adam, man is a collective term including male and female
as equally part of 'Man'.

The same truth is expressed in Genesis 2 when God speaks:

> It is not good that the man should be alone; I will make him a helper
> fit for him (v. 18).

The result is that they, man and wife, become one flesh (or
personality).

In the same early chapters the story of Cain underlines, although
negatively, the positive fact that man is made to belong to a
community. It is because this, his human birthright, is henceforth
to be no longer his, that he bursts out in anguish:

> My punishment is greater than I can bear. Behold, thou hast driven me
> this day away from the ground; and from thy face I shall be hidden;
> and I shall be a fugitive and a wanderer on the earth (Gen. 4.13-14).

The blow is a double one. He is made for fellowship with God
and his fellow man and his fate is to have neither. It is hardly
accidental that the Land of Nod means 'the Land of Wandering'.
He is the eternal fugitive.

In the earliest stories the solidarity of man with his community
and group is illustrated in such stories as that of Achan.

Because he had disobeyed the divine command which Joshua
had conveyed to the people of Israel, namely that no one should
take for himself the holy things that belong only to God because
it was he who gave the victory. So Achan must pay with his life.
This might seem harsh but at least the punishment is borne by
the wrongdoer. It is here that Eastern and Western thought part
company because the narrative continues:

> And Joshua and all Israel with him took Achan the son of Zerah, and the silver and the mantle and the bar of gold, and his sons and daughters, and his oxen and asses and sheep, and his tent, and all that he had; And they brought them up to the Valley of Achor (Trouble). . . . And all Israel stoned him with stones; and burned them with fire, and stoned them with stones (Josh. 7.*24-25*).

The person responsible for the crime is Achan yet the whole of his family including the household property are all together thought of as one social unit or personality. (See also the account of Korah's disobedience and the punishment suffered by the whole of his communal unit (Num. 16.*26, 32, 35*). Later Ezekiel protests against the individual being submerged by the community (see Ezek. 18.*2-4*).)

## KINDS OF COMMUNITY

The Hebrew idea of man as finding his true self only by belonging to a community may be illustrated by seeing the significance of the different kinds of community within which man emerges as a responsible person.

### The Community of the Family

The idea of the family is the source of the widening circles of community life and has its own beginnings in the idea of a man's house, that is, his household where he dwells with his kin. The relationship of kinship extends beyond the father's house first to other members of the family and also then to all the kinsmen who share in the privilege of being the 'people' of God.

The emphasis on the community of the family is seen in the emphasis laid on the possession of children to complete the family group.

The community has dimensions of the past, present and future.

Hence the repeated emphasis on the fact that a man at death should remain within the community of his fathers.

'Abraham breathed his last and died in a good old age, an old man and full of years, and was gathered to his people' (Gen. 25.*8*; see also Judg. 2.*10*). A similar sense of the community of the family is seen in passages where we have the idiomatic phrase 'to sleep with his fathers' as in the closing verdict upon Rehoboam (1 Kings 14.*31*). Similarly, a man belongs to those who come after him, his descendants, and the greatest disaster that could befall a Hebrew man is that there should be no continuing seed to perpetuate a man's existence through the carrying on of his name. This is the horror of Bildad's dread warning to Job, as he describes the fate of the evildoer:

> His roots dry up beneath,
>   and his branches wither above.
> His memory perishes from the earth,
>   and he has no name in the street.
> He is thrust from light into darkness,
>   and driven out of the world.
> He has no offspring or descendant among his people,
>   and no survivor where he used to live (Job 18.*16-19*).

In short, the man will not belong to the community of the family.

## The Community of the Nation

A striking feature of Hebrew thinking about the nation is that it makes no real distinction between the nation and the family. The very word used for a people or nation was used originally for kinsfolk or what we would know today as 'relatives'. Especially instructive is the opening of ch. 3 of Amos:

> Hear this word that the Lord has spoken against you, O people of Israel, against the whole family which I brought out of the land of Egypt:

'You only have I known
  of all the families of the earth;
  therefore I will punish you
  for all your iniquities' (Amos 3.*1-2*).

The use of the word 'known' in v.*2* reinforces the family idea
because it carries a sense of intimate relationship that exists within
such a community as the family. A further evidence of this
interpretation of nationhood is seen in the way that nations are
called by the names of their ancestors, as if they were large families.
So God pleads through the prophet Hosea:

What shall I do with you, O Ephraim?
  What shall I do with you, O Judah?
Your love is like a morning cloud,
  like the dew that goes early away (Hos. 6.*4*).

As if they were a single person the nation is addressed under the
name of the tribal ancestors, the founders of their family.


## The Community of the State

The recurring emphasis in the Old Testament is upon a community that is governed by God, that is a theocracy. This is the
Hebrew ideal and the state as governed by a king who is not
answerable to God is repudiated. In the world of this time, the
institution of kingship is an integral part of the city state, each
major city having its king. Yet the tone and atmosphere of Old
Testament thought is to be gauged from such passages as the
story of the Tower of Babel (Genesis 11) in which this achievement
is seen as the typical symbol of Mesopotamian pride in its culture
and as opposed to the early nomadic faith in its purity. The same
doubt about the community of the city state is expressed in the
tradition of the Israelites asking for a king, to be like other nations:

'Behold, you are old and yours sons do not walk in your ways; now appoint for us a king to govern us like all the nations'. But the thing displeased Samuel when they said, 'Give us a king to govern us' (1 Sam. 8.*5-6*).

A further protest against the city state is made by the group of extremists known as the Rechabites. In the time of Jeremiah they are used as an example of loyalty to the nomadic ideal to the rest of the nations who disobey God's word: their manifesto is given in the command of their ancestor, Rechab, on which they base their way of life:

> You shall not drink wine, neither you nor your sons for ever; you shall not build a house; you shall not sow seed, you shall not plant or have a vineyard; but you shall live in tents all your days, that you may live many days in the land where you sojourn (Jer. 35.*6-7*).

The essence of this position is a protest against the corruption of the urban civilization of the Canaanites with its city states and their kings. (See Joshua 12.*9-24*.) In time the institution of the state with a monarch became a reality and we are left with two accounts of the institution of King Saul; one favourable (1 Sam. 10.*1-10*) and one in opposition to it (1 Sam. 8.*5-20*).

Yet, although accepted under probable pressure of the imminent Philistine invasion, and in the first account represented as due to God's initiative, there are stern warnings against an imitation of the practice of the surrounding nations (1 Sam. 8.*11-17*; 1 Sam. 10.*25*). It is nearer the truth to say that the city state and the institution of kingship was more tolerated than accepted and always remained distinct from the typical, arbitrary Eastern despotism. This is the key to understanding the protest of Nathan against David (2 Sam. 12.7) and the refusal of Naboth to be dispossessed of his vineyard even by the king:

> The Lord forbid that I should give you the inheritance of my fathers (1 Kings 21.*3*).

Nowhere does the Hebrew mind accept the idea of an Eastern potentate ruling with arbitrary and despotic power. The king is the Anointed of the Lord but this means that he must serve the Lord's people.

In Israel's later thought the institution was accepted by the Hebrew mind and God is described as king, and the future saviour of Israel will be the Messianic king who will come from the royal house of David (Isaiah 11.*1*). Upon this changing attitude to the state and the monarch a penetrating comment has been made: 'Kingship in Israel is an excellent example demonstrating how an element originally foreign to Israel's national life and religious nature could be given a new meaning for the people by relating it to Israel's religion' (T. C. Vriezen, *An Outline of Old Testament Theology*, p. 220 n. 2).

The state and the monarchy remain, however, subordinate to God and they are constantly judged by the basic fact of the Old Testament, the covenant relationship between God and his people.

### THE COVENANT COMMUNITY

Behind all discussion of state and kingship as forms of community life, was the nostalgia for the relationship which existed between God and his people in the days of their desert experiences, the time of Israel's youth. This is seen as the Golden Age, when God made a covenant and Israel was faithful:

> I remember the devotion of your youth,
>     your love as a bride,
> how you followed me in the wilderness,
>     in a land not sown (Jer. *2.2;* see also Hos. *2.16-17*; *12.10*).

The attraction that remains for the Hebrew mind in the nomadic ideal is not the relative greater purity of the tribal life then but the sense of belonging to the Covenant people created by God.

The creation of his people through the initiation of his covenant is the essence of election: not because of social pressures expressed in contracts, nor by the accident of blood relationship, but by the creation of a spiritual bond and covenant.

So Abraham is spoken to by God:

> I am God Almighty; walk before me, and be blameless. And I will make my covenant between me and you, and will multiply you exceedingly. . ...
> I will give to you, and to your descendants after you, the land of your sojournings, all the land of Canaan, for an everlasting possession; and I will be their God (Gen. 17.2,8).

The emphasis is on God's initiative, the working out of his purpose. There is never any suggestion of God and his people coming together to sign a contract with the idea of doing each other some good, a mutual benefit relationship! Neither is God's election of Israel on the basis of greatness or worth; as he reminds them:

> It was not because you were more in number than any other people that the Lord set his love upon you and chose you, for you were the fewest of all peoples; but it is because the Lord loves you, and is keeping the oath which he swore to your fathers (Deut. 7.7-8).

So national superiority does not enter into it, and God continues:

> Know therefore, that the Lord your God is not giving you this good land to possess because of your righteousness; for you are a stubborn people (Deut. 9.6).

'Here it is not taught that Israel was chosen because she was better than other nations. Rather was it the miracle of Divine grace that God chose her in her weakness and worthlessness, and lavished His love upon her' (H. H. Rowley, *The Biblical Doctrine of Election*, p. 18).

From this conviction of belonging to a spiritual community

brought into being by God himself a number of far-reaching consequences follow.

First, the community founded on the initiative of God alone, cannot be limited by any barrier of territory or race. The covenant community will be judged and guided by the developing idea of what God meant by covenant. Such a spiritual community cannot be static.

Secondly, the covenant relationship and any community based upon it cannot be completely destroyed. Despite the failure of men to respond to God's initiative yet God's covenant purpose needs a community through which to be expressed and so arises the doctrine of the Remnant.

> In that day the remnant of Israel and the survivors of the house of Jacob will no more lean upon him that smote them, but will lean upon the Lord, the Holy One of Israel, in truth. A remnant will return, the remnant of Jacob, to the mighty God. For though your people Israel be as the sand of the sea, only a remnant of them will return (Is. 10.*20-22*).

Here the remnant concept speaks of judgement. Yet there is, too, the note of hope. The same voice that is heard in pronouncing the judgement of Exile yet bears witness:

> Then I will gather the remnant of my flock out of all the countries where I have driven them, and I will bring them back to their fold . . . and they shall fear no more, nor be dismayed, neither shall any be missing, says the Lord (Jer. 23.*3-4*).

Thirdly, the community based on the Covenant is a preparation for the time when the political structure of the State collapses. After the Exile, the people of Israel became even more certain that they were the People of the Covenant. Yet alongside this emphasis on their own position as the Community of the Covenant there arises the conviction that God must be the only God for men everywhere.

## MAN AND WORLD COMMUNITY

We might say that Israel through the Exile lost political status, yet in so doing she gained spiritual maturity. The State became the 'Church'. The greatest insight that led to this new interpretation of Israel's role as the Covenant Community is seen in the following passages from Second Isaiah:

> I am the Lord, I have called you in righteousness,
> I have taken you by the hand and kept you;
> I have given you as a covenant to the people,
> a light to the nations,
> to open the eyes that are blind,
> to bring out the prisoners from the dungeon,
> from the prison those who sit in darkness (Is. 42.6-7).

And the same voice continues:

> It is too light a thing that you should be my servant
> to raise up the tribes of Jacob and to restore the preserved of Israel;
> I will give you as a light to the nations,
> that my salvation may reach to the end of the earth (Is. 49.6).

In these passages the challenge to the community of the Israelites is to re-think the role and mission of such an exalted status. Chosen and elect community they indeed were—but they had to learn that their election lay in being the Servant of the whole world. Through such a mission the whole community of nations were brought within the covenant relationship—including the detested Babylonians who had subjected them to Exile! In the main, the Covenant people rejected this extension of their community of covenant and the Book of Jonah is an indictment of the nation's refusal to be the servants of anybody!

### FOR FURTHER READING

H. H. ROWLEY, *The Biblical Doctrine of Election* (Lutterworth, 1950).

L. KOEHLER, *Hebrew Man* (S.C.M., 1956).

F. MARTIN-ACHARD, *A Light to the Nations* (Oliver & Boyd, 1962).

J. PEDERSEN, *Israel, Its Life and Culture* (I-IV, Oxford, 1926).

H. H. ROWLEY, *The Missionary Message of the Old Testament* (Carey Press, 1944).

R. DE VAUX, *Ancient Israel, Its Life and Institutions* (Darton, Longman and Todd, 1961).

G. E. WRIGHT, *The Biblical Doctrine of Man in Society* (S.C.M., 1954).

PART FOUR

# GOD, MAN AND ETERNITY

# 10

# THE PROBLEM OF SUFFERING

WE HAVE considered the Bible view of God and of Man and turn now to consider the problems that arise from taking both God and man seriously. If we believe in God, who is personal, good, loving and all-powerful and also in Man who is capable of free choice and moral decisions, why is it that innocent people suffer? Doesn't God care or can he not do anything about it? Why suffering?

## THE PROBLEM EMERGING

In its most acute form the problem is raised by the affirmations of the prophets. Thus Amos insists that God is righteous and just (Amos 5.*24*). Hosea, through the break-up of his own family life, sees human sin as the estrangement of man from God (Hos. 4.*1-4*; 7.*6-8*). In Isaiah another dimension is added. God is Holy and the prophet's immediate reaction is that he is even more conscious of his own unworthiness. His sin must be purged (Is. 6). These beliefs have crystallised into a formula—or, rather, a faith— the belief in ethical monotheism. It is when we confront these beliefs about God with the known and observable facts about the distribution of suffering and sorrow, that the question is raised—

103

where is the justice and the fairness of the Lord of history? Is it not a fact that innocent people suffer and evil men get off scot-free? Why should God allow this?

## The problem articulated

In two prophets especially do we find the problem of suffering articulated. The first is Habakkuk. He is horrified by the devastation caused by the rampant Babylonian power over the subject nations. The Assyrians have been defeated at the Fall of Nineveh in 612 B.C. and all the Egyptian hopes shattered by the Chaldeans at the Battle of Carchemish in 605 B.C. Yet the Chaldeans are every bit as ruthless as the Assyrians they succeeded. The same lawless attitude of mind, the same outrage against humanity in the barbaric exhibition of sheer, sadistic power:

> At kings they scoff,
>   and of rulers they make sport.
> They laugh at every fortress,
>   for they heap up earth and take it.
> Then they sweep by like the wind and go on,
>   guilty men whose own might is their god! (Hab. 1.*10-11*).

The prophet is forced to put his dilemma into words when he records that God himself speaks against his own people:

> For lo, I am rousing the Chaldeans
>   that bitter and hasty nation,
> who march through the breadth of the earth,
>   to seize habitations not their own (Hab. 1.*6*).

What is apparent to the prophet is that although his own people are by no means guiltless, the Chaldeans, whom God is using as his instrument to chastise the Israelites, are certainly morally worse. That is, the relatively more guilty are used to punish the relatively innocent.

Thou who art of purer eyes than to behold evil
  and canst not look on wrong,
why dost thou look on faithless men,
  and art silent when the wicked swallows up
the man more righteous than he? (Hab. 1.*13*).

Why should God act in this way? 'The prophet wonders whether history does justify the righteous, or whether instead brute power is really the factor that determines men's destiny. To him it is strange that when Yahweh is the ruler of History, the Chaldeans (that is, the Babylonians) can sweep like a wild avalanche over men's lives, destroying all patterns of meaning and defying the most elementary justice' (B. W. Anderson, *The Living World of the Old Testament*, p. 322).

Without attempting a formal solution, the author does articulate the issue of innocent suffering and makes at least a worthwhile comment as he gives the reply of God to the prophet's questioning:

For still the vision awaits its time;
  it hastens to the end—it will not lie.
If it seem slow, wait for it;
  it will surely come, it will not delay.
Behold, he whose soul is not upright in him shall fail,
  but the righteous shall live by his faith (Hab. 2.*3-4*).

The prophet is pleading with his countrymen, although not able to understand the action of God, to remain loyal to God and waiting in a receptive mood for his word, to realise a sense of rich communion with God that no sense of injustice or outrage could ever destroy.

## The Confessions of Jeremiah

The same issues are brought out by the great contemporary of Habakkuk, Jeremiah, in a moving passage from his Confes-

sions. Jeremiah, a poignant figure, has often been unjustly described as a wailing, doleful character. Yet he is more truly seen as a
spiritual pioneer, of whom it has been written, 'Personal religion
becomes an established reality with Jeremiah. It is impossible to
exaggerate the wealth of the harvest that man has reaped from this
lonely seed, sown in the agony of tears and blood . . . in a very
true and profound sense, Jeremiah was the father of the saints'.
(T. H. Robinson, *Prophecy and the Prophets*, p. 140).

In a series of heart-searchings he raises the same issues as
Habakkuk:

> Righteous art thou, O Lord,
>> when I complain to thee;
> yet I would plead my case before thee.
>> Why does the way of the wicked prosper?
> Why do all who are treacherous thrive?
>> Thou plantest them, and they take root;
> they grow and bring forth fruit;
>> thou art near in their mouth
> and far from their heart.
>> But thou, O Lord, knowest me;
> thou seest me, and triest my mind toward thee.
>> Pull them out like sheep for the slaughter,
> and set them apart for the day of slaughter (Jer. 12.*1-3*).

The bitterness and sense of outraged justice is clear and the
prophet still wrestles with his misgivings as he receives God's
answer:

> If you have raced with men on foot, and they have wearied you,
>> how will you compete with horses?
> And if in a safe land you fall down,
>> how will you do in the jungle of the Jordan? (Jer. 12.*5*).

Here the prophet receives no answer but only the intensification
of the problem. The issue has now come out into the open and
no longer will it be possible for the pious to pretend that there
is no problem. (See Ps. 37.*25*.)

## THE VOCATION OF SUFFERING

A further approach to the fact of suffering and the problem that is raised by seeking to hold on to belief in the compassion and goodness of God is made through the figure of the Suffering Servant. This is the role that is given to Israel to play in the community of nations—she must be the Servant of the nations of the world and this not lightly nor easily but at the cost of undeserved suffering. The servant role is especially emphasised in the group of writings called the Servant Songs, found in Isaiah 40–55. So we read such lines as:

> But you, Israel, my servant,
>   Jacob, whom I have chosen,
> the offspring of Abraham, my friend (Is. 41.*8*).

> 'You are my witnesses,' says the Lord,
>   'and my servant whom I have chosen' (Is. 43.*10*).

> For the sake of my servant Jacob,
>   and Israel my chosen (Is. 45.*4*; see also 44.*21*; 48.*12*).

The key to these passages is the recurring parallelism between 'servant' and 'chosen'. What God is saying is that, of course, the Israelites are his elect, chosen people, and the proof of this is in the fact that they are going to be servants, not conquerors! This, says God, is what being chosen means! They are elect not to act as lords of creation but to be servants of the whole world. If this involves suffering then that is the way in which God will bring about his will. His people will respond to this as being their vocation.

Such an interpretation of what was ahead of the Hebrew nation is movingly portrayed in a series of passages which contain such insights as:

> The Lord God has given me
>   the tongue of those who are taught,

that I may know how to sustain with a word
    him that is weary.
Morning by morning he wakens, he wakens my ear,
    to hear as those who are taught.
The Lord God has opened my ear, and I was not rebellious,
    I turned not backward.
I gave my back to the smiters
    and my cheeks to those who pulled out the beard;
I hid not my face from shame and spitting (Is. 50.4-6; see also Is. 42.1-4;
    49.1-6; 52.13-53.12).

All this means that Israel will be exalted through suffering. He bears the lash of those who smite, the ignominy and shame of being publicly humiliated yet, 'In all his suffering he knows that Yahweh has chosen him to walk this *via dolorosa*, at the end of which will be vindication and exaltation. And it is through the suffering of the Servant that God inaugurates his kingdom' (B. W. Anderson, *The Living World of the Old Testament*, p. 422).

This was their call, their vocation to suffer! Their terms of reference, their manifesto is indelibly inscribed in these words:

He was despised and rejected by men;
    a man of sorrows, and acquainted with grief;
and as one from whom men hide their faces
    he was despised, and we esteemed him not (Is. 53.3).

So spake the bystanders, but they 'were not obscure persons, for the tragedy had been enacted on a vast world stage. The spectators had been kings and nations of the earth. As they watched his agonies and his death they found these suddenly illumined by an amazing significance. The great truth, then, that dawned upon mankind after the Servant's sufferings and death was just this— that these had been *vicarious* . . . while they were deriding and crushing him he was making intercession for them' (Fleming James, *Personalities of the Old Testament*, pp. 384–386).

He shall see the fruit of the travail of his soul and be satisfied;
    by his knowledge shall the righteous one, my servant,

make many to be accounted righteous;
  and he shall bear their iniquities . . .
because he poured out his soul to death,
  and was numbered with the transgressors;
yet he bore the sin of many,
  and made intercession for the transgressors (Is. 53.*11-12*).

Here is the willing acceptance of suffering not with any sense of stoic resignation but suffering that is used as an instrument to carry out the God-given vocation of his people.

Is the Servant an individual or the collective Israel? Is there a fluid point where the author moves from one to the other? Some recent words will help us! 'There are still scholars who stand by the collective interpretation but they agree that no nation, not even Israel, ever did, or perhaps ever will or can, measure up to the stature of the Servant in the Songs. Only Christ has done that' (C. R. North, *The Second Isaiah*, p. 20). Suffering on behalf of others comes to be the very means by which God reconciles the world to himself. Here is Victor not Victim:

> For the Son of man also came not to be served but to serve, and to give his life as a ransom for many (Mk. 10.*45*).

From the Suffering Servant to the Man on the Cross is but a short step.

### SUFFERING AND COMMUNION

There is another aspect of suffering that provides us with an even richer and deeper insight. Certainly, the need to justify the ways of God to men is felt acutely by the voices we have heard. Suffering is there, and men must come to terms with it. Yet what is the outcome of the suffering even of the servant? What does the experience of suffering do to man's relationship with God, to his religion? One of the greatest attempts to examine this issue

is found in the Book of Job. Job commences his dialogue with
the friends with a bitter cry:

> Let the day perish wherein I was born,
>   and the night which said,
> 'A man-child is conceived'.
>   Let that day be darkness!
>
> .    .    .    .    .    .    .
>
> Why did I not die at birth,
>   come forth from the womb and expire? (3.*3,11*).

Here is no reasoned debate but the agonising cry—why should
such things be? It has often been said that the Book of Job seeks to
solve the problem of innocent suffering, yet 'it is truer to say
that the problem of innocent suffering is used as a supremely
relevant example to examine the deeper and profounder issue of
the whole relationship between God and man. That is, the Book
of Job is about the reality or otherwise of religious faith' (E.
Jones, *The Triumph of Job*, p. 21). The outcome of the book is that
the question of the Prologue can be triumphantly answered:
'Does Job fear God for nought?' (Job 1.*9*).

After this question is put, the rest of the book is used to demon-
strate the conviction of God that in Job we have living proof of
the reality of the relationship between Job and himself. Religion
without strings is a glorious reality in the experience of Job.

Suffering is now put in its fuller context. It does not destroy
the religious bond between God and man. Although Job starts
with his impassioned outburst against his very conception and
birth, he comes through the crucible of suffering and reaches the
rich certainty of a communion with God that survives even death.

Some of the landmarks on such a spiritual journey are contained
in chapters 9, 14, 16 and 19 in which Job speaks:

> For he is not a man, as I am, that I might answer him,
>   that we should come to trial together.

There is no umpire between us,
  who might lay his hand upon us both (Job 9.*32-33*).

If a man die, shall he live again?
  All the days of my service I would wait,
till my release should come.
  Thou wouldest call, and I would answer thee;
thou wouldest long for the work of thy hands (Job 14.*14-15*).

After this brief flash of personal hope we hear again the growing
certainty that God is on his side, that is, the real God, not the
false deity of a barren orthodoxy:

O earth, cover not my blood,
  and let my cry find no resting place.
Even now, behold, my witness is in heaven,
  and he that vouches for me is on high (Job. 16.*18-19*).

For I know that my Redeemer lives,
  and at last he will stand upon the earth;
and after my skin has been thus destroyed,
  then without my flesh I shall see God,
whom I shall see on my side,
  and my eyes shall behold, and not another (Job 19.*25-27*).

Here in these passages the pilgrimage of Job is that of an innocent sufferer who is brought to a realisation of communion with
God. 'The text is silent upon the result of the encounter between
Job and God, but its certain expectation is there. It shines like a
beacon light over the tumult' (S. Terrien, *The Interpreter's Bible*,
vol. 3, pp. 1055–56). Through the very pressure of the sense of
communion with God, that no suffering can render invalid, Job
comes to believe, if only for an instant, that his communion with
God will survive death.

## FOR FURTHER READING

B. W. ANDERSON, *The Living World of the Old Testament* (Longman, rev. ed.
  1967).

E. JONES, *The Cross in the Psalms* (Independent Press, 1963).

E. JONES, *The Triumph of Job* (S.C.M., 1966).

C. R. NORTH, *The Second Isaiah* (Oxford, 1964).

H. W. ROBINSON, *The Cross in the Old Testament* (S.C.M., 1955).

I. D. SMART, *History and Theology in Second Isaiah* (Epworth 1967).

# 11

## DEATH AND THE HEREAFTER

The theme of suffering has brought us to the evident realisation
that despite suffering communion with God is possible. Fellowship between God and man can survive the experience of sorrow
and disaster, even when undeserved. All the Servant Songs, we
have seen, bear witness that such experiences can be a vocation
from God. But what about death? What happens to the communion then?

### THE DOCTRINE OF SHEOL

For the Hebrew mind, death meant the breaking up of the unity
of flesh, soul and spirit, that is, the whole person. Because they did
not make the same sharp distinction between 'life' and 'death' as
later thought, there is no question of complete extinction or
annihilation. Any sickness or weakness means a partial dying and
death itself brings a man to the point where his life is spilt like
water on the ground which cannot be gathered up again:

> We must all die, we are like water spilt on the ground, which cannot be
> gathered up again (2 Sam. 14.14).

The same metaphor is used in the Fourth Servant Song:

113

> Therefore I will divide him a portion with the great,
>   and he shall divide the spoil with the strong;
> because he poured out his soul to death (Is. 53.*12*).

After the scattering of life's powers and the break-up of one's personality, where does the 'dead person' go? The answer is 'to Sheol', the abode of the dead. It is pictured in the Old Testament as a gigantic underground cavern, which has been graphically described by many voices in the Old Testament.

Often pictured as some insatiable monster, Sheol swallows up man as in a great pit which once entered is locked fast (see Is. 5.*14*; Jonah 2.*6*). A recent description and comment has been, 'In fact, for the most part, it is a still and silent "land of forgetfulness", which even at its best is but a pale and gloomy reflection of the world of light and life which is Yahweh's special sphere' (A. R. Johnson, *The Vitality of The Individual in the Thought of Ancient Israel*, pp. 93–94).

A notable illustration of the dark dominance of this terminus of human hopes is found in the Song of Hezekiah:

> I said, In the noontide of my days I must depart:
>   I am consigned to the gates of Sheol for the rest of my years.
> I said, I shall not see the Lord in the land of the living;
>   I shall look upon man no more among the inhabitants of the world
>   (Is. 38. *10-11*).

It is true that a weak form of existence is thought of as the lot of those who go down to Sheol, as we see in the ironic account of the reception committee that awaits the tyrant who enters Sheol, the former king of Babylon:

> Sheol beneath is stirred up to meet you when you come,
>   it rouses the shades (weak shadowy ones) to greet you,
> all who were leaders of the earth; . . .
>   All of them will speak and say to you:
> 'You, too, have become as weak as we!
>   You have become like us!' (Is. 14.*9-10*; see Ezek. 32.*17ff*.).

The ultimate tragedy to the Hebrew is that in Sheol a man cannot praise God, neither can God express his covenant love for his people:

> Every day I call upon thee, O Lord;
>   I spread out my hands to thee.
> Dost thou work wonders for the dead?
>   Do the shades rise up to praise thee?
> Is thy steadfast love declared in the grave,
>   or thy faithfulness in Abaddon?
> Are thy wonders known in the darkness,
>   or thy saving help in the land of forgetfulness? (Ps. 88.9-12; see also Job 26.5).

Sheol means that the link with God is broken; neither communion nor communication is possible. Religion as we know it is over.

Although this to the devout believer is tragic enough, the original Sheol belief carries no sense of Sheol being a place of suffering and punishment.

## THE BREAK-UP OF BELIEF IN SHEOL

At first it is certain that Sheol was regarded as a territory or kingdom where God's sovereignty did not hold sway, and was withdrawn from his influence. So the Psalmist pleads for trust in God here on earth because

> The dead do not praise thee Lord,
>   nor do any that go down into silence
>   (Ps. 115.17; see also Is. 38.18; Job 14.19).

Yet to think of Death as a realm separate from the reign of the living God would be to end up in a dualistic way of thinking which would be a complete denial of what they meant by the Living God. Not for long could Yahweh remain shut out of

Sheol. Some examples of the break-through that Hebrew thought made is seen in such passages as the following:

> The Lord kills and brings to life;
>     he brings down to Sheol and raises up (1 Sam. 2.6).

So too the prophet and psalmist:

> Though they dig into Sheol,
>     from there shall my hand take them;
> though they climb up to heaven,
>     from there I will bring them down (Amos 9.2).

> Whither shall I go from thy Spirit?
>     Or whither shall I flee from thy presence?
> If I ascend to heaven, thou art there!
> If I make my bed in Sheol, thou art there! (Ps. 139.7-8).

As the sense of God's omnipotence grows and the very dynamic of the Living God is seen, it becomes increasingly impossible that God could be shut out of any part of the universe. He must be the God of the living and the dead, of heaven, earth and the underworld so that a suppliant may even cry from the depth of Sheol and know that God's dominion holds good. Such a plea is preserved in the psalm from the Book of Jonah:

> I called to the Lord, out of my distress,
>     and he answered me;
> out of the belly of Sheol I cried,
>     and thou didst hear my voice.

> .    .    .    .    .    .    .    .

> The waters closed in over me,
>     the deep was round about me;
> weeds were wrapped about my head
>     at the roots of the mountains.
> I went down to the land
>     whose bars closed upon me for ever;
> yet thou didst bring up my life from the Pit,
>     O Lord my God (Jonah 2.2,5-6).

ANTICIPATIONS OF FUTURE LIFE

Because of the very rejection of Sheol as the ending of all relationship between God and man we find that the human spirit must take its first tentative steps towards belief in a living relationship that transcends the bleak Sheol doctrine of a pale shadowy sub-life.

Of special interest is a phrase that is found three times in the following contexts:

> Enoch walked with God; and he was not, for God took him (Gen. 5.*24*).

> When they had crossed, Elijah said to Elisha, 'Ask what I shall do for you, before I am taken from you' (2 Kings 2.*9*).

> But God will ransom my soul from the power of Sheol, for he will receive me (Ps. 49.*15*).

The word for 'receive' and 'take' is the same in each instance. Yet all these passages have a link with the description of Enoch as one who did not die in the usually accepted sense. So the comment has been made, 'Nevertheless, there is so close a link of thought between these two passages in the psalms and the story of Enoch that the choice of word may be significant. Enoch was one who knew the fellowship with God in this life to such a degree that he was spared the experience of death, but was lifted into enduring fellowship' (H. H. Rowley, *The Faith of Israel*, p. 173).

Clearly there are a number of points in Hebrew thought where the affirmation is reached that Sheol is not the ultimate end. In three psalms especially is this break-through made.

*The Practice of the Presence of God—Psalm 16*

The psalmist is subject to the pressure of pagan influence to deny the very existence of the kind of God he worshipped by sharing in alien cultic activity (vv. *3-4*).

Yet he makes his testimony:

> I keep the Lord always before me;
>   because he is at my right hand,
> I shall not be moved.
>   Therefore my heart is glad and my soul rejoices;
> my body also dwells secure.
>   For thou dost not give me up to Sheol,
> or let thy godly one see the Pit (Ps. 16.*8-10*).

There are two strands in the psalmist's thought, negative and positive. Because of the bleak barrenness of the Sheol belief and also because of the certainty that nothing can intervene to destroy his fellowship with God so this pioneer voice speaks of the continuing presence of God (v.*11*).

### Intimations of Immortality—Psalm 49

This psalm seeks to wrestle with the problems of reward and retribution. What is the connection, if any, between a person's integrity and the prosperity that he knows? Is there a relation of cause and effect between a man's evil-doing and the suffering he meets?

His verdict is:

> Yea, he shall see that even the wise die,
>   the fool and the stupid alike must perish
> and leave their wealth to others.
>
> .　　　.　　　.　　　.　　　　　　　　.　　　.
>
> Man cannot abide in his pomp,
>   he is like the beasts that perish (Ps. 49.*10-12*).

So far all we see and feel is the poignancy of the human lot. A sense of futility rather than a glimpse of faith. Life ends for all, good or evil, man or beast at the same desolate place—Sheol!

So he must find some working solution to life's riddle and he does:

> Like sheep they are appointed for Sheol;
>     Death shall be their shepherd;
> straight to the grave they descend,
>     and their form shall waste away (v.*14*).

This, at least, is what happens to the wicked, but the other part of his dilemma remains! What about the end of the good man? What is going to happen to his own sense of being in communion with God? Exactly how, he does not know, but the fact of a continuing relationship he is forced to affirm:

> But God will ransom my soul from the power of Sheol,
>     for he will receive me (v.*15*).

The hope has been articulated and on this foundation men have built.


*The Great 'Nevertheless'—Psalm 73*

This psalm records the spiritual struggle of a man who seeks to retain his faith in God although he has to meet the taunts of those who say,

> 'How can God know?
>     Is there knowledge in the Most High?'
> Behold, these are the wicked;
>     always at ease, they increase in riches (Ps. *73.11-12*).

Eventually, he turns to God and in the presence of God finds some easing of his dilemma as he speaks of the outcome of evil actions.

> Until I went into the sanctuary of God;
> then I perceived their end. (v.17).

> .        .        .        .        .        .        .

> How they are destroyed in a moment,
> swept away utterly by terrors! (v.19).

So far the emphasis is on part of the problem of reward and retribution, the fate of the wicked! The answer seems to be—wait long enough and their success will prove illusory!

The other question remains—what is to become of the good, the devout? The whole psalm hinges on the opening word of verse 23 which underlines the contrasting hope of the believer in God:

> Nevertheless I am continually with thee;
> thou dost hold my right hand.
> Thou dost guide me with thy counsel,
> and afterward thou wilt receive me to glory (vv.23-24).

The very pressure of the psalmist's communion with God forces him to reject any view of Sheol that would demand him to give up such fellowship. 'The knowledge of *how* he will accomplish this remains God's secret. But the sure knowledge *that* God will act in this way suffices for him who has learned to believe in the hidden God . . . in these words is expressed hope in the consummation of his communion with God after death' (A. Weiser, *The Psalms*, p. 514).

### APOCALYPTIC AND AFTER-LIFE

As prophecy gives way to apocalyptic we find the fate of men in an after-life forms a dominant theme. As the years go by and the intervention by God in history is apparently delayed, the same moral affirmations of the prophets are now transferred to another sphere. If God is not to be seen vindicated on earth, in time, then he must gain victory over the forces of evil after this life in another sphere. These writings are often called 'apocalyptic' books, a term derived from Greek meaning 'an unveiling' or 'revelation'. A well-known example of this kind of approach is found in the Book of Revelation in the New Testament which describes the writer's vision on Patmos of the events of the last days.

Especially, in two passages that belong to apocalyptic do we find this note. They are the Isaiah Apocalypse and the Book of Daniel.

## The Isaiah Apocalypse

In a late section of the book of Isaiah, chs. 24–27 we have a block of writings that are of this apocalyptic nature, dealing with the hidden things that will be unveiled concerning the fate of the dead. Of special significance are two passages:

> He will swallow up death for ever, and the Lord God will wipe away tears from all faces, and the reproach of his people he will take away from all the earth (Is. 25.8).

> Thy dead shall live, their bodies shall rise.
> O dwellers in the dust, awake and sing for joy!
> For thy dew is a dew of light,
>     and on the land of the shades thou wilt let it fall (Is. 26.19).

The hope of some life after death now becomes articulate and resurrection of the dead, that is, the dead of Yahweh, will rise. However, this is still more a prayer with the implicit desire rather than an article of faith and certainty. Behind such an expression of religious hope is the demand that stems from prophetic teaching for justice. It is unthinkable that the ultimate fate of the Lord's 'dead', i.e. the martyrs who are faithful to Yahweh, should be identical with that of the tyrants who caused their death. Thus in both prophecy and apocalyptic, the moral claim is the same that the God of all the earth must be just and this justice must be effective, if not in this life—then in the next.

*The Daniel Apocalypse or 'Revealing'.*

In this passage the hope expressed in Isaiah 26 becomes even more a clearly articulated certainty. Under the pressure of the events of the Maccabean persecution, when the savage attack of Antiochus Epiphanes against Judaism aimed at its virtual extermination, the resistance crystallised in the revolt of Mattathias, priest of Modein, a small hill town near Jerusalem. Together with his sons, and specially Judas called the 'Hammerer' (that is, of his enemies), they formed the core of revolt. (See 1 Macc. 2.*27-28*; 2 Macc. 7.) In these struggles many were hanged and slaughtered, including a thousand loyal Jews overtaken on a Sabbath day and wiped out because they afforded no resistance! How else could the Hebrew mind deal with such facts as the triumph of the tyrants and the murder of the saints other than by reaching this certainty?

> And there shall be a time of trouble, such as never has been since there was a nation till that time; but at that time your people shall be delivered, every one whose name shall be found written in the book. And many of those who sleep in the dust of the earth shall awake, some to everlasting life and some to shame and everlasting contempt (Dan. 12.*1-2*).

The source of belief in a resurrection is faith that Yahweh must intervene to gain the victory of his own purpose. He must vindicate the triumphant loyalty of his saints in the last days.

> But the saints of the Most High shall receive the kingdom, and possess the kingdom for ever, for ever and ever (Dan. 7.*18*; see v.*27*).

### FOR FURTHER READING

W. BARCLAY (ed.) *The Bible and History* (Lutterworth, 1968).

A. R. JOHNSON, *The Vitality of the Individual in the Thought of Ancient Israel* (Univ. of Wales Press, 1949).

F. MARTIN-ACHARD, *From Death to Life* (Oliver & Boyd, 1960).

H. H. ROWLEY, *The Faith of Israel* (S.C.M., 1956)

D. S. RUSSELL, *Between the Testaments* (S.C.M. 1960).

A. WEISER, *The Psalms* (S.C.M., 1962).

# 12

# THE ULTIMATE HOPE

ONE OF the great recurring motifs of the Old Testament is the constant call to the people of Israel to remember the prior acts of God and what he has already done for them, especially in delivering them from the bondage of Egyptian oppression. This experience has clearly seared the imagination of the Hebrews.

> I am the Lord your God, who brought you out of the land of Egypt, out of the house of bondage (Ex. 20.2; see also Ex. 15.21; Ex. 19.4; Deut. 4.34).

Again and again when the prophets seek to bring back an erring nation to the way of the Lord, this is the substance of their plea—that the people should remember what God had done at this creative moment in their history (see Amos 9.7; Is. 51.10; 52.12; Hos. 11.1; Jer. 11.4). Yet this is not the only key to the interpretation of Hebrew thought. What God had done before he would do again. The prophets not only recall the past but they point forward to the future.

## THE DAY OF THE LORD

One of the most significant terms used to express this longing for a future time when God would assert his sovereignty over all human history is the 'Day of the Lord'. In the popular expectation this became a day when all the enemies of Israel would be destroyed and Israel, the Chosen People, would be exalted over the whole world. For others, a day of reckoning; for Israel, a day of vindication and triumph. The people came to believe they were exempt from the judgement invariably associated with the Day of the Lord. For them it would mean automatic approval and exaltation, just because they were a Chosen People.

This cosily comfortable doctrine was shattered by the authentic voices of the prophets:

> Woe to you who desire the day of the Lord!
>    Why would you have the day of the Lord?
> It is darkness, and not light;
>    as if a man fled from a lion,
> and a bear met him;
>    or went into the house and leaned with his hand against the wall,
> and a serpent bit him.
>    Is not the day of the Lord darkness, and not light,
> and gloom with no brightness in it? (Amos 5.*18-20*; see also Zeph. 3.*8*;
>    Is. 13.*6*; Ezek. 30.*2-3*).

What these prophets did was to deepen the significance of this popular crystallisation of Israel's hopes. The Day of the Lord certainly would bring judgement but it was to be universal and not selective. Israel, far from being exempt, would be judged even more surely because of the failure to respond to what God had done for her. There was to be no let-out clause for her.

A further consequence of this prophetic interpretation of the current popular belief in the Day of the Lord was that a new dimension was given to Israel's hope of salvation. Salvation would come but not automatically and not without suffering and judgement. Israel must learn to wait with hope and confidence:

> But they who wait for the Lord
>    shall renew their strength,

they shall mount up with wings like eagles,
    they shall run and not be weary,
they shall walk and not faint (Is. 40.*31*).


## THE MESSIANIC HOPE AND SALVATION

The classic expectation of Israel's future is expressed in the figure of the Messiah who is closely associated with the royal line of David. The term 'messiah' literally means 'anointed one' and it is used of a person set apart for a special office. It is applied to priest and prophet, to patriarch and even a foreign King (Ex. 28.*40-41*; Ps. 105.*15*; Is. 45.*1*). Yet the Messianic hope is seen in the promise made to the King David; as the chosen and anointed one of the Lord:

> And your house and your kingdom shall be made sure for ever before me;
> your throne shall be established for ever (2 Sam. 7.*16*).

As we seek to define further the Messianic Hope we shall be greatly helped if we use a hint afforded by recent scholarship: 'We might liken the whole eschatological hope (from the Greek phrase 'the last things') to a many-stranded rope. Each of the strands is an important element in its own right in the portraying of the End. Yet we do not possess a rope unless all the strands are woven together . . each of the strands of Israel's hope is inseparable from its fellows, and . . . it can only be understood in the light of the whole function of the rope'. (G. A. F. Knight, *A Christian Theology of the Old Testament*, p. 296). We shall glance briefly at various strands that make up Israel's Hope.


### The Son of David

We have already seen that the promise was made by Nathan to David that his line would be 'established for ever'. But the Davidic line is not loyal and faithful since David commits adultery, Solomon perverts Hebrew worship and Rehoboam divides the nation. Yet the succession is of God's grace not of men's blood and although the royal line is apparently destroyed the psalmist can still cry:

> Thou hast said, 'I have made a covenant with my chosen one,
>   I have sworn to David, my servant:
> "I will establish your descendants for ever
>   and build your throne for all generations" ' (Ps. 89.3-4).

## The Branch

The Fall of Jerusalem in 587 B.C. would seem to the spectator of the Hebrew nation's history the end of a dream, of their hope. But they would reckon without the faithfulness of Yahweh which is expressed in the image of the Branch:

> There shall come forth a shoot from the stump of Jesse,
>   and a branch shall grow out of his roots (Is. 11.1).

The picture is of a tree stump, dead, yet a shoot or sucker springs from below the soil and, watered by winter and spring rains, it grows with new life and hope. Jeremiah and Zechariah use a similar imagery to express their hope in God's power to fulfil his promises despite the failure of the Davidic line. (See especially Jer. 23.5; 33.15; Zech. 3.8.)

## The Royal Psalms

A third strand in what we have called this Messianic Hope is found in a number of psalms in which the central figure is some king of Israel or Judah. These psalms have been called Royal and include Pss. 2, 18, 20, 21, 45, 72, 89, 101, 110, 132 and 144.

In Ps. 2 we have a striking example of a psalm probably composed for the accession of a king of Judah in Jerusalem and used at his coronation. The king is the speaker:

> Why do the nations conspire
> and the peoples plot in vain?
> The kings of the earth set themselves,
> and the rulers take counsel together,
> against the Lord and his anointed, saying,
> 'Let us burst their bonds asunder,
> and cast their cords from us'.
> He who sits in the heavens laughs;
> the Lord has them in derision.
> Then he will speak to them in his wrath,
> and terrify them in his fury, saying,
> 'I have set my king
> on Zion, my holy hill.'
> I will tell of the decree of the Lord:
> He said to me, 'You are my son,
> today I have begotten you' (Ps. 2.1-7).

The audacity of the psalmist is breathtaking. The accession of a king of Judah, a tiny insignificant kingdom when considered against the background of the Ancient Near Eastern World, is affirmed by the psalmist to affect world history. Zion's king is the Messiah (the Anointed) of God! The underlying affirmation of the writer is that 'at the centre of history is no longer the struggle of the great world powers for existence, but God, whose relationship with worldly powers will determine their destiny' (A Weiser, *The Psalms*, p. 111). These royal psalms reflect not only the fate of the individual king but also the way in which the welfare of God's people is bound up with that of the king since he is the 'anointed' chosen representative of the chosen people. (See Pss. 84, 89). Even after the Fall of the kingdoms of Israel (722 B.C.) and Judah (587 B.C.) these psalms continue to have relevance. They are then understood to refer to the Messiah, the king who will bring salvation at the end of time.

*The Enthronement Psalms*

In a number of psalms there is a further characteristic, in that they refer to the enthronement of Yahweh as king and are probably connected with the celebration of the Feast of Tabernacles as part of the New Year ritual. Such features may be found in Pss. 47, 93 and 96–99. A significant example is found in Ps. 99 which begins:

> The Lord reigns; let the peoples tremble!
> > He sits enthroned upon the cherubim; let the earth quake!
> The Lord is great in Zion;
> > he is exalted over all the peoples.
> Let them praise thy great and terrible name!
> > Holy is he!
> Mighty King, lover of justice,
> > thou hast established equity;
> thou hast executed justice and righteousness in Jacob.
> > Extol the Lord our God;
> > worship at his footstool!
> > Holy is he! (Ps. 99.1-5).

The expectation is of a new era when Yahweh will rule the earth and the Messiah will play his part in preparing for the advent of God himself. Although as the cycle of the year comes round there is a sense in which the nation is renewed in the recurring cycle of growth and decay expressed in nature religions, here there is another factor. The memory of what God has done in the past is used to proclaim God's present and future faithfulness. At a festival in which God affirms the covenant relationship that he has with his people, the people make their response. This is the significance of the recurring refrain 'Holy is he!' in verses 3 and 5. In verse 6 of the psalm we read:

> Moses and Aaron were among his priests,
> > Samuel also was among those who called on his name.

The emphasis is upon the present tense. So we should render the opening phrase—God is become King! Once again the people of God can share in a living relationship and communion with the earth's king!

The whole psalm affirms the sure and certain hope of God's coming to rule his world and to bring in his kingdom. Such psalms in which God is enthroned as king have been well described in these words, 'In this way the House of David is reminded that it is the responsibility of the true Messiah to put an end to everything which disturbs the right relationship between the various members of society . . . this great act of worship looks forward to the day when the crisis will have been reached in the persistent struggle between the forces of light and the forces of darkness, i.e. the day when the true Messiah of the House of David, by his own dependence upon the holy Spirit and his own filial devotion to the Godhead, will have justified the decisive intervention of Yahweh, and final victory [i.e. man's full "salvation" or his enjoyment of perfect freedom] will thus be assured' (A. R. Johnson, *Sacral Kingship in Ancient Israel*, pp. 143–4).

So the Messiah will act for God in a way that God alone can effect through the gift of his spirit:

And the Spirit of the Lord shall rest upon him,
  the spirit of wisdom and understanding,
 the spirit of counsel and might,
    the spirit of knowledge and the fear of the Lord
    (Is. 11.*2*; see also such Messianic passages as Is. 9.*2-7*; Micah 5.*2-7*; Jer. 23.*5-8*; Is. 61.*1-3*).

### THE LAST THINGS AND THE COMING KINGDOM

It is in the last passage quoted from Isaiah (11.*1-9*) that we see a clear expression of eschatological expectation, that is, hope concerning the outcome of the Last Things. The characteristic feature of this messianic passage is the transfer of salvation from the earthly scene to another dimension. This is seen in the change that will come about in the natural behaviour of the animal world; there is to be a cosmic revolution in the new age:

> The wolf shall dwell with the lamb,
> and the leopard shall lie down with the kid,
> and the calf and the lion and the fatling together,
> and a little child shall lead them.
> The cow and the bear shall feed;
> their young shall lie down together;
> and the lion shall eat straw like the ox (Is. 11.6-7).

After the experience of the Exile and the delay in the advent of the Messianic King (see Malachi 1.2; 2.17) the expectation of imminent salvation gives way to the realisation that salvation would be consummated in a new era, the world to come.

This is expressed most significantly in the apocalyptic writings, specially in Daniel.

### Salvation and the Son of Man

Of the greatest relevance is the teaching concerning the Son of Man. This figure is referred to in Daniel:

> I saw in the night visions, and behold, with the clouds of heaven
> there came one like a son of man,
> and he came to the Ancient of Days
> and was presented before him.
> And to him was given dominion and glory and kingdom,
> that all peoples, nations, and languages should serve him (Dan. 7.13-14).

The ascription of 'dominion, glory and kingdom' to the Son of Man seems to be a direct reference to the Messiah. (See the apocryphal book of 1 Enoch 45.3; 51.3; 55.4, where the Messiah sits on the throne of glory.) In the same chapter, however, we read:

> And the kingdom and the dominion
> and the greatness of the kingdoms under the whole heaven

shall be given to the people of the saints of the Most High;
> their kingdom shall be an everlasting kingdom,
and all dominions shall serve and obey them (Dan. 7.27).

Both 'Son of Man' and 'the saints of the Most High' are to
gain dominion. The Hebrew mind has no difficulty in speaking of
one and many at the same time and we may very well have a
further example of corporate personality. (See, for example,
Is. 53 and the Suffering Servant.)

Certainly in a later period in such works as the Similitudes of
Enoch (1 Enoch 37–71) and also in the New Testament the Son
of Man figures centrally as the Messiah. In the New Testament
we find such a term used of Jesus himself and it is a self-
designation. (See Mk. 10.45; Is. 53.5,12.)

In one sense in him, the King, the Kingdom has come. This has
been called 'realised eschatology'—'the arrival already of the last
things'. (See C. H. Dodd, *The Parables of the Kingdom.*)

So we reach the end of this sketch of Old Testament theology
with the certainty of the coming Kingdom. It has still to come
fully, but there is no doubt in this faith of the Hebrews, because
'Eschatology is the expression of the belief that God holds history
in the hollow of His hand, and that He will make the history of
the world end in complete communion between God and man,
so that He will become King; or in other words, so that He may be
all in all' (T. C. Vriezen, *An Outline of Old Testament Theology*,
p. 371).

## FOR FURTHER READING

C. F. Barth, *Introduction to the Psalms* (Blackwell, 1966).
A. R. Johnson, *Sacral Kingship in Ancient Israel* (Univ. of Wales Press, 2nd
ed. 1967).
J. Muilenberg, *The Way of Israel* (Routledge & Kegan Paul, 1962).
H. Ringgren, *The Messiah in the Old Testament* (S.C.M., 1956).

# PRINCIPAL PERIODS OF HEBREW HISTORY

# INDEX